PENGUIN BOOKS — GREAT IDEAS

The Prince

Niccolò Machiavelli

1469–1527

Niccolò Machiavelli

The Prince

TRANSLATED BY GEORGE BULL

PENGUIN BOOKS — GREAT IDEAS

PENGUIN BOOKS

Published by the Penguin Group
Penguin Books Ltd, 80 Strand, London WC2R ORL, England
Penguin Group (USA) Inc., 375 Hudson Street, New York, New York 10014, USA
Penguin Books Australia Ltd, 250 Camberwell Road,
Camberwell, Victoria 3124, Australia
Penguin Books Canada Ltd, 10 Alcorn Avenue, Toronto, Ontario, Canada M4V 3B2
Penguin Books India (P) Ltd, 11 Community Centre,
Panchsheel Park, New Delhi – 110 017, India
Penguin Group (NZ), Cnr Airborne and Rosedale Roads,
Albany, Auckland 1310, New Zealand
Penguin Books (South Africa) (Pty) Ltd, 24 Sturdee Avenue,
Rosebank 2196, South Africa

Penguin Books Ltd, Registered Offices: 80 Strand, London WC2R ORL, England

www.penguin.com

Il Principe first published 1531–2
This translation first published in Penguin Classics 1961
Reprinted with revisions 1975, 1981, 1995, 1999
This edition published in Penguin Books 2004

2

Translation copyright © George Bull, 1961, 1975, 1981, 1995, 1999
All rights reserved

Taken from the Penguin Classics edition of *The Prince*, translated with notes by
George Bull and with an introduction by Anthony Grafton

The moral right of the translator has been asserted

Set in Monotype Dante
Typeset by Rowland Phototypesetting Ltd, Bury St Edmunds, Suffolk
Printed in England by Clays Ltd, St Ives plc

Except in the United States of America, this book is sold subject
to the condition that it shall not, by way of trade or otherwise, be lent,
re-sold, hired out, or otherwise circulated without the publisher's
prior consent in any form of binding or cover other than that in
which it is published and without a similar condition including this
condition being imposed on the subsequent purchaser

Letter from Niccolò Machiavelli to the Magnificent Lorenzo dé Medici

Men who are anxious to win the favour of a Prince nearly always follow the custom of presenting themselves to him with the possessions they value most, or with things they know especially please him; so we often see princes given horses, weapons, cloth of gold, precious stones, and similar ornaments worthy of their high position. Now, I am anxious to offer myself to Your Magnificence with some token of my devotion to you, and I have not found among my belongings anything as dear to me or that I value as much as my understanding of the deeds of great men, won by me from a long acquaintance with contemporary affairs and a continuous study of the ancient world; these matters I have very diligently analysed and pondered for a long time, and now, having summarized them in a little book, I am sending them to Your Magnificence.

And although I consider this work unworthy to be put before you, yet I am fully confident that you will be kind enough to accept it, seeing that I could not give you a more valuable gift than the means of being able in a very short space of time to grasp all that I, over so many years and with so much affliction and peril, have learned and understood. I have not embellished or crammed this book with rounded periods or big, impressive words, or with any blandishment or superfluous decoration of the kind which many are in the habit of using to describe or adorn what they have produced; for my ambition has been either that nothing should distinguish my book, or that it should find favour solely through the variety of its contents and the seriousness of its subject-matter. Nor I hope will it be considered presumptuous for a man of low and humble status to dare discuss and lay down the law about how princes should rule; because, just as men who are sketching the landscape put themselves down in the plain to study the nature of the mountains and the highlands, and to study the low-lying land they put themselves high on the mountains, so, to comprehend fully the nature of the people, one must be a prince, and to comprehend fully the nature of princes one must be an ordinary citizen.

So, Your Magnificence, take this little gift in the spirit in which I send it; and if you read and consider it diligently, you will discover in it my urgent wish that you reach the eminence that fortune and your other qualities promise you. And if, from your lofty peak, Your Magnificence will sometimes glance down to these low-lying regions, you will realize the extent to which, undeservedly, I have to endure the great and unremitting malice of fortune.

The Prince

I

How many kinds of principality there are and the ways in which they are acquired

All the states, all the dominions under whose authority men have lived in the past and live now have been and are either republics or principalities. Principalities are hereditary, with their prince's family long established as rulers, or they are new. The new are completely new, as was Milan to Francesco Sforza, or they are like limbs joined to the hereditary state of the prince who acquires them, as is the kingdom of Naples in relation to the king of Spain. Dominions so acquired are accustomed to be under a prince, or used to freedom; a prince wins them either with the arms of others or with his own, either by fortune or by prowess.

II

Hereditary principalities

I shall leave out any discussion of republics, since I discussed them at length on another occasion. I shall deal only with the principality, and I shall follow the order set out above, and debate how these principalities can be governed and maintained.

I say, then, that in hereditary states, accustomed to their prince's family, there are far fewer difficulties in maintaining one's rule than in new principalities; because it is enough merely not to neglect the institutions founded by one's ancestors and then to adapt policy to events. In this way, if the prince is reasonably assiduous he will always maintain his rule, unless some extraordinary and inordinate force deprive him of it; and if so deprived, whenever the usurper suffers a setback he will reconquer.

We have in Italy, for example, the duke of Ferrara, he could not withstand the assaults of the Venetians in '84, nor those of Pope Julius in 1510, but for other reasons than that he had been long established. The fact is that the natural prince has less reason and less need to give offence; and so it follows that he should be more loved; and if he does not provoke hatred by extraordinary vices, it stands to reason that his subjects should naturally be well disposed towards him. And in the antiquity and persistence of his rule memories of innovations and the reasons for them disappear; because one change always leaves a toothing-stone for the next.

III
Composite principalities

But in the new principality difficulties do arise. First, if it is not entirely new but a new appendage to an old state (so that the territory as a whole can be called composite) disorders arise chiefly because of one natural difficulty always encountered in new principalities. What happens is that men willingly change their ruler, expecting to fare better. This expectation induces them to take up arms against him; but they only deceive themselves, and they learn from experience that they have made matters worse. This follows from another common and natural necessity: a prince is always compelled to injure those who have made him the new ruler, subjecting them to the troops and imposing the endless other hardships which his new conquest entails. As a result you are opposed by all those you have injured in occupying the principality, and you cannot keep the friendship of those who have put you there; you cannot satisfy them in the way they had taken for granted, yet you cannot use strong medicine on them, as you are in their debt. For always, no matter how powerful one's armies, in order to enter a country one needs the goodwill of the inhabitants. It was for these reasons that Louis XII, king of France, speedily occupied Milan and speedily lost it. On the first occasion Ludovico's own forces were enough to take the city from him, because the people who had opened the gates to him, finding they had deceived themselves in their expectations and as regards the benefits they had anticipated, could not stand the affronts they received from the newcomer.

It is certainly true that when lands that have rebelled are reconquered they are not lost so easily; for the ruler, taking advantage of the revolt, is less scrupulous in securing himself by punishing the offenders, probing suspects, strengthening himself where he is weakest. Thus for France to lose Milan all that had to happen the first time was that a Duke Ludovico should rampage on the borders, but for France to lose it a second time the whole world had to oppose her, and her armies had to be destroyed or chased out of Italy; and the reasons for this I gave above. None the less, both times France lost Milan.

The general reasons for the first loss have been discussed. It remains now to give those for the second, and to see what remedies were available to the king of France, and what steps could have been taken by someone in the same straits to maintain his conquest more securely than he did. Now I say that those states which when acquired are joined to a state long held by the conqueror are either of the same country, sharing the same language, or they are not. When they are, it is a very easy matter to hold on to them, especially when they are not used to freedom; and to hold them securely it is enough to have destroyed the line of the former ruling prince. For the rest, so long as their old ways of life are undisturbed and there is no divergence in customs, men live quietly: as we have seen in the case of Burgundy, Brittany, Gascony, and Normandy, which have been with France for so long. Although here there is some divergence in language, none the less their customs are similar, and they can easily get along together. If the ruler wants to keep hold of his new possessions, he must bear two things in mind: first, that the family of the old prince must be destroyed; next, that he must change neither their laws nor their taxes. In this way, in a very short space of time the new principality will be rolled into one with the old.

But when states are acquired in a province differing in language, in customs, and in institutions, then difficulties arise; and to hold them one must be very fortunate and very assiduous. One of the best, most effective expedients would be for the conqueror to go to live there in person. This course of action would make a new possession more secure and more permanent; and this was what the Turk achieved in Greece. For all the other measures he took, had he not gone to settle there he would have found it impossible to hold that state. Being on the spot, one can detect trouble at the start and deal with it immediately; if one is absent, it is discerned only when it has grown serious, and it is then too late. And besides, this policy prevents the conquered territory from being plundered by one's officials. The subjects are satisfied because they have direct recourse to the prince; and so they have more reason to love him, if they want to be good, and to fear him, if they want to be otherwise. Anyone wishing to invade the state has to think twice about it. So if he settles there the ruler can lose his new state only with the greatest difficulty.

The other superior expedient is to establish settlements in one or two places; these will, as it were, fetter the state to you. Unless you establish settlements, you will have to garrison large numbers of mounted troops and infantry. Settlements do not cost much, and the prince can found them and maintain them at little or no personal expense. He injures only those from whom he takes land and houses to give to the new inhabitants, and these victims form a tiny minority, and can never do any harm since they remain poor and scattered. All the others are left undisturbed, and so should stay quiet, and as well as this they are frightened to do wrong lest what happened to the dispossessed should happen to them. To sum up, settlements are economical and more faithful, and do less harm; and those who are injured cannot hurt you because, as I said, they are scattered and poor. And here it has to be noted that men must be either pampered or crushed, because they can get revenge for small injuries but not for grievous ones. So any injury a prince does a man should be of such a kind that there is no fear of revenge. If, however, instead of establishing settlements the prince sends in troops, expenses are far higher, as all the revenues have to be devoted to defence and the gain becomes a loss. The prince does far more injury, because he harms the whole state by billeting his army in different parts of the country, everyone suffers from this annoyance, and everybody is turned into an enemy. And those who grow hostile can do him harm, because they remain, defeated, in their own homes. In every way, therefore, this means of defence is as useless as colonization is useful.

In addition, anyone in a country which differs from his own in the way I described should make himself the leader and protector of the smaller neighbouring powers, and he should endeavour to weaken those which are strong. He should also take precautions to check an invasion of the province by a foreigner as powerful as himself. Invariably, the intruder will be brought in by those who are disaffected, because of excessive ambition or because of fear. Thus the Aetolians once brought the Romans into Greece; and in every other country they invaded, the Romans were brought in by the inhabitants. This is what happens: as soon as a powerful foreigner invades a country all the weaker powers give him their support, moved by envy of the power which has so far dominated them. So, as far as these weaker powers are concerned, he has no trouble at all in winning them to his side, because of their own accord they straight away merge with the state he establishes. All he has to watch is that they do not build up too much strength and too much authority; and with his own strength and their support he can easily hold down those who are powerful and so make himself, in everything, the master of the country. Whoever does not attend carefully to these points will quickly lose what he has acquired; even while he still holds on he will experience countless difficulties and annoyances.

The Romans, in the countries they seized, did watch these matters carefully. They established settlements, supported the weaker powers without increasing their strength, crushed the powerful, and did not allow any powerful foreigner to win prestige. The country of Greece provides a good enough example. Here, the Romans supported the Achaeans and the Aetolians; they crushed the Macedonian kingdom; and they drove out Antiochus. They never allowed the Achaeans or the Aetolians to expand their territories however well they behaved; they never allowed Philip to persuade them into an alliance without holding him down; and despite his power, Antiochus was never granted any authority in Greece. In these instances, the Romans did what all wise rulers must: cope not only with present troubles but also with ones likely to arise in future, and assiduously forestall them. When trouble is sensed well in advance it can easily be remedied; if you wait for it to show itself any medicine will be too late because the disease will have become incurable. As the doctors say of a wasting disease, to start with it is easy to cure but difficult to diagnose; after a time, unless it has been diagnosed and treated at the outset, it becomes easy to diagnose but difficult to cure. So it is in politics. Political disorders can be quickly healed if they are seen well in advance (and only a prudent ruler has such foresight); when, for lack of a diagnosis, they are allowed to grow in such a way that everyone can recognize them, remedies are too late.

So the Romans saw when troubles were coming and always took counter-measures. They never, to avoid a war, allowed them to go unchecked, because they knew that there is no avoiding war; it can only be postponed to the advantage of others. They made up their minds to wage war with Philip and Antiochus in Greece, in order not to have to do so in Italy. At the time they could have avoided doing either, but they would not. Nor were the Romans ever tempted to do what we hear every day on the lips of the wise men of our generation, to make the most of the present time; rather, they made the most of their own prowess and prudence. Time sweeps everything along and can bring good as well as evil, evil as well as good.

But let us go back to France, and see if that country has adopted any of the measures I have been discussing. I shall talk about Louis, not Charles, and so about a man whose career it has been possible to study more closely because he was entrenched in Italy for a longer time. You will see how Louis has done the opposite of what ought to be done to maintain one's rule in an alien country.

King Louis was brought into Italy by the ambition of the Venetians, who wanted by this means to win for themselves half Lombardy. I do not mean to condemn the course of action taken by the king; he wanted to get a footing in Italy, he had no allies there – on the contrary because of the actions of King Charles all the gates were barred to him – and so he was forced to make friends where he could. His policy in this matter would even have proved successful, provided he had not gone wrong elsewhere. Now, when Lombardy fell into his hands the king immediately regained the standing which Charles had lost. Genoa capitulated; the Florentines became his allies; the marquis of Mantua, the duke of Ferrara, the Bentivogli, the countess of Forlì, the rulers of Faenza, of Pesaro, of Rimini, of Camerino, of Piombino, the citizens of Lucca, Pisa, Siena, all came forward to seek his friendship. Then the Venetians were in a position to realize how rash they had been. In order to gain two towns in Lombardy they had made him, the king, ruler of a third of Italy.

Now consider with what little trouble the king could have maintained his standing in Italy, if he had observed the rules I gave above and kept all those allies of his safe and secure. There were many of them, and they were weak and frightened, some of the Church, some of the Venetians; so they were bound to stay by him, and through them he could easily have safeguarded himself against the powers which remained strong. But no sooner was he in Milan than he did the contrary, helping Pope Alexander to occupy the Romagna. Nor did he realize that by taking this decision he weakened himself, alienated his allies and those who had thrown themselves into his arms, and strengthened the Church by adding so much temporal power to its existing spiritual power, which gives it such authority. Having made one mistake, he was forced to make others. To frustrate the ambition of Alexander and prevent his becoming ruler of Tuscany he was forced to come down into Italy himself. Not content with having made the Church powerful and having alienated his allies, he then, because he wanted the kingdom of Naples, divided it with the king of Spain. Whereas to start with he was master of Italy he now brought in a rival to whom the ambitious and the discontented might have recourse. He could have left in Naples a king who was in his pay. Instead he expelled him to put in his place one who could chase him out in turn.

The wish to acquire more is admittedly a very natural and common thing; and when men succeed in this they are always praised rather than condemned. But when they lack the ability to do so and yet want to acquire more at all costs, they deserve condemnation for their mistakes. If France could have attacked Naples with her own forces, she should have done so; if not, she should not have divided it. And if the partition of Lombardy with the Venetians could be excused, because it gave Louis a foothold in Italy, the other partition deserved to be condemned, because there was no such necessity for it.

Louis had, therefore, made these five mistakes: he had destroyed the weaker powers; increased the power of someone already powerful in Italy; brought into that country a very powerful foreigner; stayed away from Italy himself; failed to establish settlements there. Even these mistakes, if he had lived, need not have been fatal if there had not been a sixth: his dispossessing the Venetians of their state. If he had not made the Church strong, or brought Spain into Italy, it would have been reasonable and necessary to crush the Venetians. But having taken those steps, he should never have let them be ruined; because while they remained powerful they would always have prevented the others from moving against Lombardy. The Venetians would have opposed this unless it gave them control of Lombardy themselves, and the others would not have wanted to wrest it from France to give it to them. Nor would they have had the courage to defy both France and the Venetians. If anyone should say that King Louis ceded the Romagna to Alexander and the kingdom of Naples to Spain in order to escape a war, I would reply with the arguments used above, that one must never allow disorder to continue so as to escape a war. Anyhow one does not escape: the war is merely postponed to one's disadvantage. And if anyone should cite the king's good faith, which he had pledged to the pope, and his promise to undertake that enterprise in return for having his marriage dissolved and a cardinal's hat given to Rouen, my reply is what I shall say later concerning the good faith of princes and the way they should keep their word. King Louis, therefore, lost Lombardy because he observed none of the rules observed by others who have seized countries and determined to hold on to them. There is nothing fantastic about this, it is very commonplace and reasonable. I had a word on this subject with Rouen, at Nantes, when Valentino (as Cesare Borgia, son of Pope Alexander, was popularly called) was occupying the Romagna. When the cardinal of Rouen said to me that the Italians did not understand war, I retorted that the French did not understand statecraft, because, if they understood it, then they would not let the Church become so great. And the course of events in Italy has shown how the greatness of the Church and of Spain has been caused by France, and how the ruin of France has been caused by them. From this we can deduce a general rule, which never or rarely fails to apply: that whoever is responsible for another's becoming powerful ruins himself, because this power is brought into being either by ingenuity or by force, and both of these are suspect to the one who has become powerful.

IV

Why the kingdom of Darius conquered by Alexander did not rebel against his successors after his death

One could well wonder, after having considered all the difficulties involved in holding a newly acquired state, how it was that when Alexander, who had in a few years become ruler of all Asia, died with his conquest scarcely completed, there was not, as might have been expected, a general uprising. Instead, Alexander's successors ruled securely; and in their government the only difficulty arose from their own ambitions and rivalries. My answer to this problem is that all principalities known to history are governed in one of two ways, either by a prince to whom everyone is subservient and whose ministers, with his favour and permission, help govern, or by a prince and by nobles whose rank is established not by favour of the prince but by their ancient lineage. Such nobles have states and subjects of their own, and these acknowledge them as their lords and bear a natural affection towards them. In states governed by a prince and his servants, the prince has greater authority. For throughout the whole country he alone is recognized as being entitled to allegiance; anyone else is obeyed as a minister and an official for whom no special love is felt.

Contemporary examples of these two different kinds of government are provided by the Turk and the king of France. The Turkish empire is ruled by one man; all the others are his servants. This one ruler divides the empire into *sandjaks*, in charge of which he places various administrators, whom he changes and varies as it suits him. But the king of France is surrounded by a long-established order of nobles, who are acknowledged in France by their own subjects and are loved by them. They have their prerogatives; the king cannot take these away from them except at his own peril. So, to make a comparison between these two kinds of state, it is difficult to win control of the Turkish empire but, once it has been conquered, it can be held with ease. On the other hand, in several respects you will find that the French state can be more easily seized, but it can be held only with great difficulty.

The reasons for it being difficult to succeed in winning possession of the Turkish empire are that there is no chance of being called in by the local princes, and that one cannot hope to forward the enterprise by the rebellion of those who are near to the ruler. And this is because of the reasons I gave above: they are all slaves bound in loyalty to their master and so it is more difficult to corrupt them; and even should they be corrupted one cannot hope to make much use of them because they are unable, for the reasons already given, to draw the people after them. Whoever attacks the Turkish empire, therefore, must expect to find it completely united, and he is constrained to base his hopes on his own strength rather than his enemy's disunity. But if once the Turk has been vanquished and broken in battle so that he cannot raise new armies, there is nothing to worry about except the ruler's family. When that has been wiped out there is no one left to fear, because the others have no credit with the people; and just as before his victory the conqueror has nothing to hope from them, so afterwards he need not fear them.

The opposite happens in kingdoms governed in the way France is. You can easily invade if you win over one of the barons. There always exist malcontents and those who want a change. These, for the reasons explained, can open up the state to you and facilitate your victory. But subsequently, when you want to maintain your rule, you run into countless difficulties, as regards both those who have helped you and those you have subjugated. Nor is it enough for you to destroy the ruler's family, because there still remain nobles to raise insurrections; and being able neither to satisfy them nor to destroy them you lose the state as soon as their opportunity presents itself.

Now, if you will consider the kind of government which Darius administered, you will find it resembled that of the Turk; and so first of all Alexander had to attack him head-on and drive him from the field. Then, after he had won that victory and Darius was dead, the state rested securely in Alexander's hands for the reasons discussed above. Had they been united, his successors could have enjoyed it undisturbed; certainly, there were no tumults other than those they themselves provoked. But as for states constituted like France, it is impossible to rule them with so little trouble. This fact explains the many rebellions against the Romans in Spain, France, and Greece, which were due to the number of principalities of which these countries were composed. The Romans were always unsure of their hold while the memory of these principalities endured. But when Roman rule had been long established and had become powerful, and the principalities were completely forgotten, the Romans consolidated their position. Later on, however, when they, the Romans, fought among themselves, each one of them could draw support from various parts of the conquered territories in proportion to the authority he had acquired; allegiance was given to the Romans individually because the families of the former rulers had been wiped out. So if this is borne in mind no one will wonder at the ease with which Alexander kept command of Asia, or at the difficulties encountered by others, such as Pyrrhus and many more like him, in maintaining their conquests. This contrast does not depend on whether the conquerors are more or less capable but on the kind of state they conquer.

v

How cities or principalities which lived under their own laws should be administered after being conquered

When states newly acquired as I said have been accustomed to living freely under their own laws, there are three ways to hold them securely: first, by devastating them; next, by going and living there in person; thirdly, by letting them keep their own laws, exacting tribute, and setting up an oligarchy which will keep the state friendly to you. In the last case, the government will know that it cannot endure without the friendship and power of the prince who created it, and so it has to exert itself to maintain his authority. A city used to freedom can be more easily ruled through its own citizens, provided you do not wish to destroy it, than in any other way.

Examples are provided by the Spartans and the Romans. The Spartans ruled Athens and Thebes through the oligarchies they established there, although in the end they lost them. The Romans, in order to hold Capua, Carthage, and Numantia, destroyed them, and so never lost them. They wanted to rule Greece almost as the Spartans did, freely, under its own laws, but they did not succeed; so in order to maintain their power they were constrained to destroy many cities in that province. Indeed, there is no surer way of keeping possession than by devastation. Whoever becomes the master of a city accustomed to freedom, and does not destroy it, may expect to be destroyed himself; because, when there is a rebellion, such a city justifies itself by calling on the name of liberty and its ancient institutions, never forgotten despite the passing of time and the benefits received from the new ruler. Whatever the conqueror's actions or foresight, if the inhabitants are not dispersed and scattered, they will forget neither that name nor those institutions; and at the first opportunity they will at once have recourse to them, as did Pisa after having been kept in servitude for a hundred years by the Florentines. But when cities or provinces are used to living under a prince, and his family is wiped out, since on the one hand they are used to obeying, and on the other have lost their former prince, they cannot agree on the choice of a new prince from among themselves and they cannot live in freedom without one. So they are slower to take up arms, and a prince can win them and assure himself of them more easily. But in republics there is more life, more hatred, a greater desire for revenge; the memory of their ancient liberty does not and cannot let them rest; in their case the surest way is to wipe them out or to live there in person.

VI
New principalities acquired by one's own arms and prowess

No one should be surprised if, in discussing states where both the prince and the constitution are new, I shall give the loftiest examples. Men nearly always follow the tracks made by others and proceed in their affairs by imitation, even though they cannot entirely keep to the tracks of others or emulate the prowess of their models. So a prudent man must always follow in the footsteps of great men and imitate those who have been outstanding. If his own prowess fails to compare with theirs, at least it has an air of greatness about it. He must behave like those archers who, if they are skilful, when the target seems too distant, know the capabilities of their bow and aim a good deal higher than their objective, not in order to shoot so high but so that by aiming high they can reach the target.

I say, therefore, that in completely new states, where the prince himself is a newcomer, the difficulty he encounters in maintaining his rule is more or less serious insofar as he is more or less able. And since the very fact that from being a private citizen he has become a prince presupposes either ability or good fortune, it would seem that one or the other of these should to some extent lessen many of the difficulties encountered. None the less, the less a man has relied on fortune the stronger he has made his position. It also helps if the prince has no other states and so is forced to live in his new state in person. But to come to those who became princes by their own abilities and not by good fortune, I say that the most outstanding are Moses, Cyrus, Romulus, Theseus, and others like them. Although one should not reason about Moses, since he merely executed what God commanded, yet he must be praised for the grace which made him worthy of speaking with God. But let us consider Cyrus and the others who acquired and founded kingdoms: they were all praiseworthy, and their actions and institutions, when examined, do not seem to differ from those of Moses, who had such a mighty teacher. And when we come to examine their actions and lives, they do not seem to have had from fortune anything other than opportunity. Fortune, as it were, provided the matter but they gave it its form; without opportunity their prowess would have been extinguished, and without such prowess the opportunity would have come in vain.

Thus for the Israelites to be ready to follow Moses, in order to escape from servitude, it was necessary for him to find them, in Egypt, enslaved and oppressed by the Egyptians. For Romulus to become king of Rome and founder of his country, he had to have left Alba and been exposed to die when he was born. Cyrus needed to find the Persians rebellious against the empire of the Medes, and the Medes grown soft and effeminate through the long years of peace. Theseus could not have demonstrated his prowess had he not found the Athenians dispersed. The opportunities given them enabled these men to succeed, and their own exceptional prowess enabled them to seize their opportunities; in consequence their countries were ennobled and enjoyed great prosperity.

Men who become rulers by prowess similar to theirs acquire their principalities with difficulty but hold them with ease. The difficulties they encounter in acquiring their principalities arise partly because of the new institutions and laws they are forced to introduce in founding the state and making themselves secure. It should be borne in mind that there is nothing more difficult to handle, more doubtful of success, and more dangerous to carry through than initiating changes in a state's constitution. The innovator makes enemies of all those who prospered under the old order, and only lukewarm support is forthcoming from those who would prosper under the new. Their support is lukewarm partly from fear of their adversaries, who have the existing laws on their side, and partly because men are generally incredulous, never really trusting new things unless they have tested them by experience. In consequence, whenever those who oppose the changes can do so, they attack vigorously, and the defence made by the others is only lukewarm. So both the innovator and his friends come to grief. But to discuss this subject thoroughly we must distinguish between innovators who stand alone and those who depend on others, that is between those who to achieve their purposes can force the issue and those who must use persuasion. In the second case, they always come to grief, having achieved nothing; when, however, they depend on their own resources and can force the issue, then they are seldom endangered. That is why all armed prophets have conquered, and unarmed prophets have come to grief. Besides what I have said already, the populace is by nature fickle; it is easy to persuade them of something, but difficult to confirm them in that persuasion. Therefore one must urgently arrange matters so that when they no longer believe they can be made to believe by force. Moses, Cyrus, Theseus, and Romulus would not have been able to have their institutions respected a long time if they had been unarmed, as was the case in our time with Frà Girolamo Savonarola who came to grief with his new institutions when the crowd started to lose faith in him, and he had no way of holding fast those who had believed or of forcing the incredulous to believe. Men such as he have considerable difficulty in achieving their ends, and the most dangerous time for them is when they are still striving; but once they have succeeded and begin to be venerated, having destroyed those who were envious of their abilities, they stay powerful, secure, respected, and happy.

I want now to add another, lesser example to these lofty ones. It will, however, bear the comparison to some extent, and I shall let it stand for others of its kind. The example I have in mind is Hiero of Syracuse. From being a private citizen, he became ruler of Syracuse. He too owed nothing to fortune except his opportunity, because the Syracusans chose him to lead their army when they were being driven hard, and then he earned the right to be their prince. His prowess was such, even when he was an ordinary citizen, that his biographer wrote: '*quod nihil illi deerat ad regnandum praeter regnum*'.* He disbanded the old militia and organized a new one; he abandoned former alliances and made fresh ones; and when he had his own alliances and troops he had the foundations for whatever he wanted. Hiero, therefore, had to work very hard to establish his position, but very little to maintain it.

VII
New principalities acquired with the help of fortune and foreign arms

Private citizens who become princes purely by good fortune do so with little exertion on their own part; but subsequently they maintain their position only by considerable exertion. They make the journey as if they had wings; their problems start when they alight. This is the case with men who either buy their way into power or are granted it by the favour of someone else, as happened with many in Greece, in the cities of Ionia and

---

* 'That he had all the attributes of a king except a kingdom.'

the Hellespont, who were made satraps by Darius so that they might rule those cities for his security and glory. This was also the case with those who from being private citizens became emperors by corrupting the soldiers. Such rulers rely on the goodwill and fortune of those who have elevated them, and both these are capricious, unstable things. They do not know how to maintain their position, and they cannot do so. They do not know how, because, unless they possess considerable talent and prowess, private citizens are incapable of commanding; they cannot, because they do not have loyal and devoted troops of their own. Then again, governments set up overnight, like everything in nature whose growth is forced, lack strong roots and ramifications. So they are destroyed in the first bad spell. This is inevitable unless those who have suddenly become princes are of such prowess that overnight they can learn how to preserve what fortune has suddenly tossed into their laps, and unless they can then lay foundations such as other princes would have already been building on.

Of these two ways of becoming a prince, by prowess or by fortune, I want now to give two examples from living memory: namely Francesco Sforza and Cesare Borgia. Francesco, using the right means, and by his own great prowess, from being a private citizen became duke of Milan. What he won only after endless struggles he then held with little exertion. On the other hand, Cesare Borgia, commonly called Duke Valentino, acquired his state through the good fortune of his father, and lost it when that disappeared; and this happened even though he used the same ways and means any prudent and capable prince would to consolidate his power in the states he had won by the arms and fortune of others. As I said before, a man of exceptional prowess can build the foundations of his state after he has acquired it, even if by doing so he runs a risk himself as well as endangering the whole subsequent edifice. So if we consider the duke's career as a whole, we find that he laid strong foundations for the future. And I do not consider it superfluous to discuss these, because I know no better precepts to give a new prince than ones derived from Cesare's actions; and if what he instituted was of no avail, this was not his fault but arose from the extraordinary and inordinate malice of fortune.

Alexander VI, when he sought the aggrandizement of his son, faced a considerable number of actual and potential difficulties. First, he saw no way of acquiring a state for the duke, unless it were one of the states of the Church; but he knew the duke of Milan and the Venetians would never consent if he set out to seize one of these. Faenza and Rimini were already under the protection of the Venetians. He saw as well that the Italian arms, or such of them as he could hope to utilize, were controlled by those who had reason to fear the aggrandizement of the pope; he could not trust himself to them, since they belonged to the Orsini and the Colonna and their confederates. What he had to do, therefore, was to create disorder, throwing their states into a turmoil, so that he could win secure control of part of them. This proved very easy to do because he found the Venetians, for other reasons, endeavouring to bring the French back into Italy. Not only did Alexander

not gainsay this, he facilitated it by dissolving King Louis'
former marriage. So the king invaded Italy with the help
of the Venetians and the consent of Alexander, and he
was no sooner in Milan than the pope had troops from
him for the Romagna campaign; and the Romagna
yielded to him because of the standing of the king in
Italy. But then when the duke had won the Romagna,
and the Colonna had been crushed, two things prevented
him from consolidating his position and advancing
further: first, the loyalty of his troops was doubtful, and
second, there was the policy of France. To explain this,
it seemed that the Orsini troops, of which he had made
use, might betray him, not only halting his progress
but robbing him of what he had won; and it seemed that
the king might do the same. He had one confirmation
of these fears when, after the capture of Faenza, he
assaulted Bologna and saw the Orsini troops go into
battle half-heartedly. As for the king, the duke realized
what was in his mind when, after capturing the duchy
of Urbino, he invaded Tuscany and the king called him
off. So the duke determined to rely no longer on the
arms and fortune of others. First he undermined the
power of the Orsini and Colonna factions in Rome,
winning the allegiance of all their high-born adherents
by giving them offices and commissions, and honouring
them according to their rank. The upshot was that within
a few months their attachment to the factions was
destroyed and they were all for the duke. After this he
waited his chance to destroy the leaders of the Orsini,
having already dispersed those of the Colonna. A good
opportunity came his way, and he used it well. What

happened was that the Orsini realized, belatedly, that the aggrandizement of the duke and of the Church spelled their own ruin, and therefore they summoned a conference at Magione near Perugia. Out of this meeting came the revolt of Urbino, uprisings in the Romagna, and countless dangers to the duke. He overcame all of these with the help of the French. His former standing in Italy was restored, but he no longer trusted France or the forces of others, and in order not to run risks by doing so he turned to stratagem. His powers of dissimulation were so great that even the Orsini, through Signor Paulo, reconciled themselves with him. The duke used every device of diplomacy to reassure Paulo, giving him gifts of money, clothes, and horses; and so their simplicity led the Orsini to Sinigaglia, into his hands. So, the leaders destroyed, their followers were forced into the duke's camp. The duke had laid excellent foundations for his future power. He held all the Romagna with the duchy of Urbino, and, above all, he seemed to have won the trust and friendship of the Romagna and its inhabitants, now that they had started to prosper under his rule.

As this point deserves close study and imitation by others, I will not leave it out. Now, the duke won control of the Romagna and found that it had previously been ruled by weak overlords, quicker to despoil their subjects than to govern them well. They had given them cause for anarchy rather than union, to such an extent that the province was rife with brigandage, factions, and every sort of abuse. He decided therefore that it needed good government to pacify it and make it obedient to the sovereign authority. So he placed there messer Remirro de Orco, a cruel, efficient man, to whom he entrusted the fullest powers. In a short time this Remirro pacified and unified the Romagna, winning great credit for himself. Then the duke decided that there was no need for this excessive authority, which might grow intolerable, and he established in the centre of the province a civil tribunal, under an eminent president, on which every city had its own representative. Knowing also that the severities of the past had earned him a certain amount of hatred, to purge the minds of the people and to win them over completely he determined to show that if cruelties had been inflicted they were not his doing but prompted by the harsh nature of his minister. This gave Cesare a pretext; then, one morning, Remirro's body was found cut in two pieces on the piazza at Cesena, with a block of wood and a bloody knife beside it. The brutality of this spectacle kept the people of the Romagna at once appeased and stupefied.

But let us go back to where we were before that digression. The duke found himself in a position of considerable power and, in part, safe against immediate threats, through possessing his own troops and having largely destroyed the forces of those who were near enough to do him harm. Then, wanting to expand further, he still had to go carefully regarding France, because he knew this would not have been allowed by the king, who had belatedly realized his mistaken policy. So Cesare started to seek new alliances and to temporize with France when her troops were on the expedition towards Naples directed against the Spaniards who were besieging Gaeta. His intention was to secure Spanish support; and he would have had immediate success, if Alexander had lived.

Those were his plans regarding the immediate future. Beyond that, his chief cause for anxiety was that the next successor to the papacy might prove unfriendly and might endeavour to take back what Alexander had given him. He sought to guard against this eventuality in four ways: by destroying all the families of the rulers he had despoiled, thus depriving the pope of the opportunity of using them against him; second, by winning over all the patricians in Rome, as I mentioned before, in order to hold the pope in check; third, by controlling the College of Cardinals as far as he could; fourth, by acquiring so much power himself before Alexander died that he could on his own withstand an initial attack. Of these four, he had, on the death of Alexander, accomplished three; and he had almost accomplished the fourth. He killed as many of the rulers he had despoiled as he could reach, and very few escaped; he had won over the Roman patricians, and he had a very large following in the College. As for extending his power, he had aimed at becoming the ruler of Tuscany. Perugia and Piombino he already possessed, Pisa was under his protection. And as soon as he need have no concern over France (he no longer had to, the French having already lost the kingdom of Naples to the Spaniards, with the result that both sides sought to buy his friendship) he would have pounced on Pisa. That done, Lucca and Siena would have surrendered at once, partly from spite towards the Florentines, and partly through fear; and the Florentines were at his mercy. Had he succeeded in all this (as he would have succeeded in the year that Alexander died) he would have acquired such strength and prestige that he would have been able to stand alone and been dependent no longer on the fortune and strength of others but on his own power and prowess. But Alexander died five years from the time Cesare took up the sword. He left him with his state in the Romagna consolidated but with everything else in the air, between two extremely powerful and hostile armies, and mortally ill. The duke was a man of such ferocity and prowess, and he understood so well that men must be either won over or destroyed, and the foundations he laid in so short a time were so sound, that, had those armies not been bearing down on him, or had he been in good health, he would have overcome every difficulty. The strength of the foundations he laid is evident: because the Romagna waited for him for over a month; in Rome, even when he was more dead than alive, he was unmolested, and although the Baglioni, the Vitelli, and the Orsini entered the city they roused no one against him; if he could not make whom he wanted pope, he was at least able to keep the papacy from going to one he did not want. If, when Alexander died, he had been well himself, everything would have been easy for him. And he himself said to me, the day Julius II was elected, that he had thought of everything that could happen when his father died, and found a remedy for everything except that he never thought that when he did so he himself would also be at the point of death.

So having summed up all that the duke did, I cannot possibly censure him. Rather, I think I have been right in putting him forward as an example for all those who have acquired power through good fortune and the arms of others. He was a man of great courage and high intentions, and he could not have conducted himself other than the way he did; his plans were frustrated only because Alexander's life was cut short and because of his own sickness. So a new prince cannot find more recent examples than those set by the duke, if he thinks it necessary to secure himself against his enemies, win friends, conquer either by force or by stratagem, make himself both loved and feared by his subjects, followed and respected by his soldiers, if he determines to destroy those who can and will injure him, to reform ancient institutions, be severe yet loved, magnanimous and generous, and if he decides to destroy disloyal troops and create a new standing army, maintaining such relations with kings and princes that they have either to help him graciously or go carefully in doing him harm. The duke deserves censure only regarding the election of Pope Julius, where he made a bad choice. As I said, not being able to get a pope to his liking he could have kept the papacy from going to one who was not; and he should never have allowed the election of one of those cardinals he had injured, or one who would have cause to fear him. Men do you harm either because they fear you or because they hate you. Those to whom Cesare himself had done harm were, among others, San Pietro ad Vincula, Colonna, San Giorgio, Ascanio. All the others, were they to be elected, had cause to fear him, except for Rouen and the Spaniards. The Spaniards in the College were Cesare's countrymen, and under an obligation to him; Rouen was powerful in his own right, having the backing of the kingdom of France. The duke's aim, first and foremost, should have been to get a Spaniard elected pope and, failing that, to let it be Rouen, not San Pietro ad Vincula. Whoever believes that with great men new services wipe out old injuries deceives himself. So the duke's choice was a mistaken one; and it was the cause of his ultimate ruin.

VIII
Those who come to power by crime

As there are also two ways of becoming a prince which cannot altogether be attributed either to fortune or to prowess, I do not think I ought to leave them out, even though one of them can be dealt with at greater length under the heading of republics. The two I have in mind are when a man becomes prince by some criminal and nefarious method, and when a private citizen becomes prince of his native city with the approval of his fellow citizens. In dealing with the first method, I shall give two examples, one from the ancient world, one from the modern, without otherwise discussing the rights and wrongs of this subject, because I imagine that these examples are enough for anyone who had to follow them.

Agathocles, the Sicilian, not only from the status of a private citizen but from the lowest, most abject condition of life, rose to become king of Syracuse. At every stage of his career this man, the son of a potter, behaved like a criminal; none the less he accompanied his crimes with so much audacity and physical courage that when he joined the militia he rose through the ranks to become praetor of Syracuse. After he had been appointed to this position, he determined to make himself prince and to possess by force and without obligation to others what had been voluntarily conceded to him. He reached an understanding about this ambition of his with Hamilcar the Carthaginian, who was campaigning with his armies in Sicily. Then one morning he assembled the people and Senate of Syracuse, as if he meant to raise matters which affected the republic; and at a prearranged signal he had all the senators, along with the richest citizens, killed by his soldiers; and when they were dead he seized and held the government of that city, without encountering any other internal opposition. Although he was twice routed and finally besieged by the Carthaginians, not only did he successfully defend the city, but, leaving some of his troops to defend it, he invaded Africa with the rest, and in a short time lifted the siege and reduced the Carthaginians to severe straits. They were compelled to make a pact with him, contenting themselves with the possession of Africa and leaving Sicily to Agathocles. So whoever studies that man's actions and life will discover little or nothing that can be attributed to fortune, inasmuch as not by anyone's favour he rose through the ranks of the militia, as I said, and his progress was attended by countless difficulties and dangers; that was how he won his principality, and he maintained his position with many audacious and dangerous enterprises. Yet it cannot be called prowess to kill fellow-citizens, to betray friends, to be treacherous, pitiless, irreligious. These ways can win a prince power but not glory. One can draw attention to the prowess of Agathocles in confronting and surviving danger, and his courageous spirit in enduring and overcoming adversity, and it appears that he should not be judged inferior to any eminent commander; none the less, his brutal cruelty and inhumanity, his countless crimes, forbid his being honoured among eminent men. One cannot attribute to fortune or prowess what was accomplished by him without the help of either.

In our own time, during the pontificate of Alexander VI, there was Oliverotto of Fermo. Years before, he had been left fatherless as a small boy and was brought up by a maternal uncle called Giovanni Fogliani. In his early youth he was sent to serve as a soldier under Paulo Vitelli so that he could win high command after being trained by him. When Paulo died, Oliverotto soldiered under Vitellozzo, his brother; and in a very short time, as he was intelligent, and a man of courage and audacity, he became Vitellozzo's chief commander. But he thought it was servile to take orders from others, and so he determined that, with the help of some citizens of Fermo to whom the enslavement of their native city was more attractive than its liberty, and with the favour and help of Vitellozzo, he would seize Fermo for himself. He wrote to Giovanni Fogliani saying that, having been many years away from home he wanted to come and see him and his city and to make some investigation into his own estate. He had worked for nothing else except honour, he went on, and in order that his fellow citizens might see that he had not spent his time in vain, he wanted to come honourably, with a mounted escort of a hundred companions and servants. He begged Giovanni to arrange a reception which would bring honour to Giovanni as well as to himself, as he was Giovanni's foster child. Giovanni failed in no duty of hospitality towards his nephew. He had him honourably welcomed by the citizens of Fermo and lodged him in his own mansion. There, after a few days had passed during which he waited in order to complete the secret arrangements for his future crime, Oliverotto prepared a formal banquet to which he invited Giovanni Fogliani and the leading citizens of Fermo. After they had finished eating and all the other entertainment usual at such banquets was done with, Oliverotto artfully started to touch on subjects of grave importance, talking of the greatness of Pope Alexander and of Cesare his son, and of their enterprises. When Giovanni and the others began to discuss these subjects in turn, he got to his feet all of a sudden, saying that these were things to be spoken of somewhere more private, and he withdrew to another room, followed by Giovanni and all the other citizens. And no sooner were they seated than soldiers appeared from hidden recesses, and killed Giovanni and all the others. After this slaughter, Oliverotto mounted his horse, rode through the town, and laid siege to the palace of the governing council; consequently they were frightened into obeying him and into setting up a government of which he made himself the prince. And having put to death all who, because they would resent his rule, might injure him, he strengthened his position by founding new civil and military institutions. In this way, in the space of the year that he held the principality, he not only established himself in the city of Fermo but also made himself formidable to all the neighbouring states. His overthrow would have proved as difficult as that of Agathocles, if he had not let himself be tricked by Cesare Borgia when, at Sinigaglia, as was recounted above, Cesare trapped the Orsini and Vitellozzo Vitelli. Oliverotto was also trapped there, and a year after committing parricide he, along with Vitellozzo, the teacher as regards both his prowess and his crimes, was strangled.

One might well wonder how it was that Agathocles (and others like him) after countless treacheries and cruelties, could live securely in his own country and hold foreign enemies at bay, with never a conspiracy against him by his countrymen, inasmuch as many others, because of their cruel behaviour, have not been able to maintain their rule even in peaceful times, let alone in the uncertain times of war. I believe that here it is a question of cruelty used well or badly. We can say that cruelty is used well (if it is permissible to talk in this way of what is evil) when it is employed once for all, and one's safety depends on it, and then it is not persisted in but as far as possible turned to the good of one's subjects. Cruelty badly used is that which, although infrequent to start with, as time goes on, rather than disappearing, grows in intensity. Those who use the first method can, with God and with men, somewhat enhance their position, as did Agathocles; the others cannot possibly stay in power.

So it should be noted that when he seizes a state the

new ruler must determine all the injuries that he will need to inflict. He must inflict them once for all, and not have to renew them every day, and in that way he will be able to set men's minds at rest and win them over to him when he confers benefits. Whoever acts otherwise, either through timidity or misjudgement, is always forced to have the knife ready in his hand and he can never depend on his subjects because they, suffering fresh and continuous violence, can never feel secure with regard to him. Violence must be inflicted once for all; people will then forget what it tastes like and so be less resentful. Benefits must be conferred gradually; and in that way they will taste better. Above all, a prince must live with his subjects in such a way that no development, either favourable or adverse, makes him vary his conduct. For, when adversity brings the need for it, there is no time to inflict harm; and the favours he may confer are profitless, because they are seen as being forced, and so they earn no thanks.

IX
The constitutional principality

But now we come to the other case, where a private citizen becomes the ruler of his country neither by crime nor by any other outrageous act of violence but by the favour of his fellow-citizens (and this we can call a constitutional principality, to become the ruler of which one needs neither prowess alone nor fortune, but rather a lucky astuteness). I say that one becomes a prince in this case with the favour of the people or of the nobles. These two different dispositions are found in every city; and the people are everywhere anxious not to be dominated or oppressed by the nobles, and the nobles are out to dominate and oppress the people. These opposed ambitions bring about one of three results; a principality, a free city, or anarchy.

A principality is created either by the people or by the nobles, according to whether the one or the other of these two classes is given the opportunity. What happens is that when the nobles see they cannot withstand the people, they start to increase the standing of one of their own numbers, and they make him prince in order to be able to achieve their own ends under his cloak. The people in the same way, when they see they cannot withstand the nobles, increase the standing of one of themselves and make him prince in order to be protected by his authority. A man who becomes prince with the help of the nobles finds it more difficult to maintain his position than one who does so with the help of the people. As prince, he finds himself surrounded by many who believe they are his equals, and because of that he cannot command or manage them the way he wants. A man who becomes prince by favour of the people finds himself standing alone, and he has near him either no one or very few not prepared to take orders. In addition, it is impossible to satisfy the nobles honourably, without doing violence to the interests of others; but this can be done as far as the people are concerned. The people are more honest in their intentions than the nobles are, because the latter want to oppress the people, whereas they want only not to be oppressed. Moreover, a prince can never make himself safe against a hostile people: there are too many of them. He can make himself safe against the nobles, who are few. The worst that can happen to a prince when the people are hostile is for him to be deserted; but from the nobles, if hostile, he has to fear not only desertion but even active opposition. The nobles have more foresight and are more astute, they always act in time to safeguard their interests, and they take sides with the one whom they expect to win. Again, a prince must always live with the same people, but he can well do without the nobles, since he can make and unmake them every day, increasing and lowering their standing at will.

To clarify the discussion further, I say that there are two main considerations to be remembered in regard to the nobles: either they conduct themselves in such a way that they come to depend entirely on your fortunes, or they do not. Those who become dependent, and are not rapacious, must be honoured and loved; those who remain independent of you do so for two different reasons. They may do so because they are pusillanimous and naturally lacking in spirit; if so you should make use of them, especially those who are capable of giving sensible advice, since they will respect you when you are doing well, and you will have nothing to fear from them in times of adversity. But when they deliberately and for reasons of ambition remain independent of you, it is a sign that they are more concerned about themselves than about you. Against nobles such as these, a prince must safeguard himself, fearing them as if they were his declared enemies, because in times of adversity they will always help to ruin him.

A man who is made a prince by the favour of the people must work to retain their friendship; and this is easy for him because the people ask only not to be oppressed. But a man who has become prince against the will of the people and by the favour of the nobles should, before anything else, try to win the people over; this too is easy if he takes them under his protection. When men receive favours from someone they expected to do them ill, they are under a greater obligation to their benefactor; just so the people can in an instant become more amicably disposed towards the prince than if he had seized power by their favour. And there are many ways in which a prince can win them over. These vary according to circumstances, so no definite rule can be given and I shall not deal with them here. I shall only conclude that it is necessary for a prince to have the friendship of the people; otherwise he has no remedy in times of adversity.

Nabis, prince of the Spartans, withstood the whole of Greece and a triumphant Roman army, and successfully defended his country and his own authority against them. All he had to do, when danger threatened, was to take steps against a few of his subjects; but this would not have been enough had the people been hostile to him. Let no one contradict this opinion of mine with that trite proverb, that he who builds on the people builds on mud. That may be so when a private citizen bases his power on the people and takes it for granted that the people will rescue him if he is in danger from enemies or from the magistrates. (In this case, he could often find he had made a mistake, as happened with the Gracchi in Rome and messer Giorgio Scali in Florence.) But if it is a prince who builds his power on the people, one who can command and is a man of courage, who does not despair in adversity, who does not fail to take precautions, and who wins general allegiance by his personal qualities and the institutions he establishes, he will never be let down by the people; and he will be found to have established his power securely.

Principalities usually come to grief when the transition is being made from limited power to absolutism. Princes taking this step rule either directly or through magistrates. In the latter case, their position is weaker and more dangerous, because they rely entirely on the will of those citizens who have been put in office; and these, especially in times of adversity, can very easily depose them either by positive action against them or by not obeying them. And when danger comes, the prince has no time to seize absolute authority, because the citizens and subjects, accustomed to taking orders from the magistrates, will not take them from him in a crisis. In disturbed times, also, men whom the prince can trust will be hard to find. So such a prince cannot rely on what he has experienced in times of tranquillity, when the citizens have need of his government. When things are quiet, everyone dances attendance, everyone makes promises, and everybody would die for him so long as death is far off. But in times of adversity, when the state has need of its citizens, there are few to be found. And this test of loyalty is all the more dangerous since it can be made only once. Therefore a wise prince must devise ways by which his citizens are always and in all circumstances dependent on him and on his authority; and then they will always be faithful to him.

X

How the strength of every principality should be measured

There is another consideration rightly to be borne in mind when inquiring into the characteristics of these principalities: and that is whether a prince has territory such that, in case of necessity, he can stand alone, or whether he must always have recourse to the protection of others. To clarify this further, I say that, in my judgement, those princes can stand alone who have sufficient manpower or money to assemble an army equal to an encounter with any aggressor. In the same way, those princes must always have recourse to others who cannot take the field against the enemy but are forced to retreat behind walls and make their defence there. I have discussed the first case already, and later on I shall say whatever occurs to me on that subject. As for the second case, nothing can be said except to advise such princes to strengthen and fortify their own towns and not to worry about the country around. If a prince has fortified his town well, and has arranged his government in the way I said (and I shall say more about this), then an enemy will be very circumspect in attacking him. Men always dislike enterprises where the snags are evident, and it is obviously not easy to assault a town which has been made into a bastion by a prince who is not hated by the people.

The cities of Germany are wholly independent, they control only limited territory, and obey the emperor only when they want to. They fear neither him nor any neighbouring power, because they are so fortified that everyone knows it would be a protracted, difficult operation to reduce them. This is because they all have excellent moats and walls; they have adequate artillery; they always lay in public stocks of drink, food, and fuel to last a year. Over and above this, every German city, making provision for the common people without public loss, always keeps a year's supply of the wherewithal for them to work at those trades which give them their livelihood and are the sinews of the city itself. Military exercises always enjoy a high standing, and they have many laws and institutions providing for them.

Therefore a prince who has a well-fortified city and does not make himself hated is secure against attack; yet even if there were an attack, the besieger would have to abandon the enterprise with ignominy, because the course of events is so variable that no one can stay encamped with his army, in idleness, for a year. One might well object: if the people have their possessions outside the walls of the city and see them being burned, they will not be able to contain themselves, and the length of the siege and their own self-interest will make them forget their duty to the prince. My answer to this is that a powerful, courageous prince will always be able to overcome all such difficulties, inspiring his subjects now with the hope that the ills they are enduring will not last long, now with fear of the enemy's cruelty, and taking effective measures against those who are too outspoken. In addition, the enemy will as a matter of course burn and pillage the countryside when he arrives, and he will do this at a time when the prince's subjects are still fired with enthusiasm for the defence, so the prince has all the less reason to worry, because by the time this enthusiasm has died down, the losses will already have been sustained and the damage done, and there will be no remedy for it. So the subjects will identify themselves even more with their prince, since now that their houses have already been burned and their lands pillaged in his defence they will consider that there is a strong bond of obligation on his part. The nature of man is such that people consider themselves put under an obligation as much by the benefits they confer as by those they receive. So, bearing all this in mind, it should not be difficult for a prudent prince to inspire his subjects with determination during a siege, so long as he has adequate provisions and means of defence.

XI
Ecclesiastical principalities

It now remains to discuss ecclesiastical principalities; and here the difficulties which have to be faced occur before the ruler is established, in that such principalities are won by prowess or by fortune but are kept without the help of either. They are maintained, in fact, by religious institutions, so powerfully mature that, no matter how the ruler acts and lives, they safeguard his government. Ecclesiastical princes alone possess states, and do not defend them; subjects, and do not govern them. And though their states are not defended they are not taken away from them; and their subjects, being without government, do not worry about it and neither can nor hope to overthrow it in favour of another. So these principalities alone are secure and happy. But as they are sustained by higher powers which the human mind cannot comprehend, I shall not argue about them; they are exalted and maintained by God, and so only a rash and presumptuous man would take it on himself to discuss them. None the less if anyone should ask me how it is that the Church has attained such great temporal power, inasmuch as, up to the time of Alexander, the Italian potentates, and not only those who are called potentates but every baron and nobleman, even the pettiest, set it at naught, but now a king of France trembles before it, and it has been able to chase him out of Italy and ruin the Venetians, I should not think it superfluous to recall to some extent how it happened, even though the story is well known.

Before Charles, king of France, invaded Italy, that country was ruled by the pope, the Venetians, the king of Naples, the duke of Milan, and the Florentines. These powers necessarily had two main preoccupations: the one, that no armed foreign power should invade Italy; the other, that no one power among themselves should enlarge its dominion. Those who had especially to be watched were the pope and the Venetians. To hold the

Venetians in check, an alliance of all the others was necessary, as was the case in the defence of Ferrara; and to pin down the pope use was made of the Roman barons. As these were split into two factions, Orsini and Colonna, there was always scope for dissension between them; and while they remained armed before the very eyes of the pontiff they kept the papacy weak and insecure. Although sometimes a spirited pope, such as Sixtus, might come along, even such a man could never rid himself of this nuisance, for all his good fortune or statecraft. This was because of the brevity of a pope's reign. In the ten years that, on average, a pope ruled, he scarcely had time to crush one of the factions; and then, for example, if one pope had almost managed to destroy the Colonna, another came along hostile to the Orsini (so ensuring the resurgence of the Colonna), and yet did not have time enough to destroy the Orsini.

This meant that the temporal power of the pope was little respected in Italy. But then came the reign of Alexander VI, and he, more than any other pontiff who has ever lived, showed how much a pope could achieve with money and armed force. With Duke Valentino as his instrument and the invasion by the French as his occasion, he brought about all those things I discussed above regarding the duke's activities. Although his aim was the aggrandizement of the duke, not of the Church, none the less what he did increased the greatness of the Church; and after his death, when the duke had been destroyed, the Church inherited the fruits of his labours. Then came Pope Julius. He found the Church already great, possessing the Romagna, with the Roman barons destroyed and, as a result of Alexander's vigour, the factions wiped out; and he also found ready to hand a means of accumulating wealth which had not been employed before Alexander. Julius not only continued but also improved on all these things. He planned to win Bologna for himself and to crush the Venetians and to chase the French out of Italy. He succeeded in all his enterprises, and earned all the more credit in as much as he did everything for the aggrandizement of the Church and not for that of any individual. He also kept the Orsini and Colonna factions in the same condition as he had found them. And although among these there were some leaders disposed to make trouble, two things held them in check: the one, the greatness of the Church, which overawed them; the other, their being without cardinals, who cause the tumults among them. These factions will never stay quiet when they have their own cardinals, because the latter stir up feuds, both in Rome and outside, and those barons are bound to come to the aid of their own side; and so conflicts and tumults among the barons are provoked by the ambition of the prelates. Now, His Holiness Pope Leo found the papacy in an extremely strong position; and it is our hope that, his immediate predecessors having established its greatness by force of arms, he, by his goodness and countless other virtues, will make it very great and revered.

XII

Military organization and mercenary troops

Having discussed in detail all the characteristics of the
principalities I listed to start with, and having to some
extent considered the reasons why they prosper or fail,
and shown the methods often used to acquire and retain
them, it now remains for me to discuss in general the
various ways in which these principalities can organize
themselves for attack or defence. We said above that a
prince must build on sound foundations; otherwise he is
bound to come to grief. The main foundations of every
state, new states as well as ancient or composite ones,
are good laws and good arms; and because you cannot
have good laws without good arms, and where there are
good arms, good laws inevitably follow, I shall not
discuss laws but give my attention to arms.

Now, I say that the arms on which a prince bases the
defence of his state are either his own, or mercenary, or
auxiliary, or composite. Mercenaries and auxiliaries are
useless and dangerous. If a prince bases the defence of
his state on mercenaries he will never achieve stability
or security. For mercenaries are disunited, thirsty for
power, undisciplined, and disloyal; they are brave among
their friends and cowards before the enemy; they have
no fear of God, they do not keep faith with their fellow
men; they avoid defeat just so long as they avoid battle;
in peacetime you are despoiled by them, and in wartime
by the enemy. The reason for all this is that there is no
loyalty or inducement to keep them on the field apart

from the little they are paid, and this is not enough to make them want to die for you. They are only too ready to serve in your army when you are not at war; but when war comes they either desert or disperse. I should have little need to labour this point, because the present ruin of Italy has been caused by nothing else but the reliance placed on mercenary troops for so many years. Although there were times when some made good use of them, and they appeared brave enough when matched against other mercenaries, when the foreigner invaded Italy they showed themselves for what they were. So it was that Charles, king of France, was able to conquer Italy with his billeting officers alone. And he who said that the reasons for this were our own sins was telling the truth; but they were those I have described, not the sins he thought. As they were sins committed by princes, they too have paid the penalty for them.

I want to show more clearly what unhappy results follow the use of mercenaries. Mercenary commanders are either skilled in warfare or they are not: if they are, you cannot trust them, because they are anxious to advance their own greatness, either by coercing you, their employer, or by coercing others against your own wishes. If, however, the commander is lacking in prowess, in the normal way he brings about your ruin. If anyone argues that this is true of any other armed force, mercenary or not, I reply that armed forces must be under the control of either a prince or a republic: a prince should assume personal command and captain his troops himself; a republic must appoint its own citizens, and when a commander so appointed turns out incompetent, should change him, and if he is competent, it should limit his authority by statute. Experience has shown that only princes and armed republics achieve solid success, and that mercenaries bring nothing but loss; and a republic which has its own citizen army is far less likely to be subjugated by one of its own citizens than a republic whose forces are not its own.

Rome and Sparta endured for many centuries, armed and free. The Swiss are strongly armed and completely free. The Carthaginians provide an example of reliance on mercenary arms in ancient times. They were very nearly subjugated by their mercenary troops, after the first war with the Romans was over, even though their own citizens held the positions of command. After the death of Epaminondas, the Thebans put Philip of Macedon in command of their army; and when he had won a victory he robbed them of their liberty. After the death of Duke Filippo, the Milanese hired Francesco Sforza to soldier for them against the Venetians; and when he had defeated the enemy at Caravaggio he joined forces with them in order to subjugate his employers, the Milanese themselves. Sforza, his father, after being hired by Queen Joanna of Naples, deserted her without warning and left her defenceless; so to save her kingdom she was compelled to throw herself on the mercy of the king of Aragon. Admittedly, the Venetians and the Florentines have in the past used mercenary arms to extend their power, and their commanders have fought to defend them, without however seizing the state. But my comment on this is that here the Florentines happen to have been lucky. As for the good commanders likely to cause them anxiety, one has failed to achieve military success, one has been checked in his designs, another has directed his ambition elsewhere. Giovanni Acuto was the one who proved unsuccessful, and, as that was so, his loyalty could not be put to the test; but everyone will admit that if he had been successful in battle the Florentines would have been in his power. The Sforzas always had the Bracceschi against them, and they held each other in check. Francesco directed his ambition towards Lombardy, Braccio against the Church and the kingdom of Naples.

But let us have a look at what happened a little while ago. As their commander the Florentines appointed Paulo Vitelli, a very shrewd man who, starting modestly, achieved considerable standing. Had he taken Pisa the Florentines would undeniably have had to fall in with his wishes, because if he had gone over to their enemies they would have been powerless against him; and keeping him in their service meant that they had to obey him. If the expansion of Venice is considered, it will be seen that the Venetians won glory for themselves and remained secure when they made war with their own forces (this was before they started to campaign on the mainland); with their own patricians and citizen army they displayed the greatest prowess. But when they started to fight on the mainland they lost this prowess and fell in with the military traditions of Italy. When they first started to acquire territory on the mainland they did not have much to fear from their commanders, as their dominions were still very limited and their standing was considerable. But when they expanded, with Carmagnola as their commander, they tasted the error of their ways. They had seen the great prowess of which Carmagnola was capable, and under his leadership they had defeated the duke of Milan. Then they perceived that he was only lukewarm in his conduct of the war and they realized that he would win no more battles for them; but they could not afford to dismiss him, lest they lost what they had acquired. So, for safety's sake, they were forced to kill him. They then appointed as their commanders Bartolommeo da Bergamo, Ruberto da San Severino, the count of Pitigliano, and men such as these; and when they were in command the question was whether the Venetians could hold on to what they had rather than whether they could hope for new gains. Such was the position at Vailà where, in one day's engagement, they lost what it had taken them eight hundred years' exertion to conquer. Mercenary armies bring only slow, belated, and feeble conquests, but sudden, startling defeat. Since these examples have brought me to Italy, which for so many years has been dominated by mercenary arms, I would like to discuss them more thoroughly. If their origins and development have been made clear, it will be easier to provide a remedy.

You must realize that as soon as in more recent times Italy started to repudiate the Empire, and the standing of the papacy became higher in the temporal sphere, the country split into several states. What happened was that in many of the big cities there were uprisings against the nobles who had formerly, with the backing of the emperor, held them in subjection; and the Church, in order to increase its temporal authority, supported these revolts. In many other cities one of the citizens became prince. So Italy came to be almost entirely under the control of the Church and some few republics, and then, as the priests and townsmen had no experience in military matters, they started to hire foreign troops. The first to win a standing for this kind of army was Alberigo da Conio, of Romagna. From his school came, among others, Braccio and Sforza, who in their time were the masters of Italy. Then there followed all those other mercenaries up to our own times. And the result of their prowess has been that Italy has been overrun by Charles, plundered by Louis, occupied by Ferdinand, and out-raged by the Swiss. It has been the policy of these mercenaries first to detract from the military standing of infantry in order to increase that of their own troops. They did this because, as they were stateless men soldier-ing for money, leadership of a few infantry troops did not give them any standing, while they could not provide adequately for large numbers. So they had recourse to cavalry, and in this way they were honoured and adequately provided for, while needing only tolerable numbers. Things came to such a pass that in an army of twenty thousand soldiers there would be hardly two thousand infantry. Beyond this, they directed all their efforts to ridding themselves and their soldiers of any cause for fear or need of exertion; instead of fighting to the death in their scrimmages they took prisoners, without demanding ransom. They never attacked garri-son towns by night; and if they were besieged they never made a sortie; they did not bother to fortify their camps with stockades or ditches; they never campaigned in winter. All these things were permissible under their military code, and this policy was followed by them so that, as I said, they might escape both exertion and danger: and as a result they have led Italy into slavery and ignominy.

XIII
Auxiliary, composite, and native troops

Auxiliaries, the other useless kind of troops, are involved when you call upon a powerful state to come to your defence and assistance. Pope Julius did this in the recent past, when, having seen the sad account given of themselves by his mercenaries in the Ferrara campaign, he turned to auxiliaries and arranged for Ferdinand of Spain to assist him with his men and troops. In themselves, auxiliary forces can prove useful and reliable, but for the one who calls them in they are almost always a disaster. You are left in the lurch if they are defeated, and in their power if they are victorious. Although ancient history is full of examples, none the less I will be content with the fresh example provided by Pope Julius II. His course of action could not have been more ill-considered when, wanting to take Ferrara, he threw himself into the hands of a foreigner. But such was his good fortune that something else happened which prevented his reaping what he had sown: after his auxiliaries were routed at Ravenna, the Swiss arrived on the scene and drove the victors off, so that to everyone's surprise, including his own, Julius escaped being at the mercy of the enemy (as they had

Niccolò Machiavelli

fled) or being in the power of his own auxiliaries (as he had not conquered with their arms). The Florentines, being completely without forces, hired ten thousand Frenchmen to reduce Pisa; because of which decision they incurred more dangers than at any time during their troubles. The emperor of Constantinople, to withstand his neighbours, sent into Greece ten thousand Turks who, when the war was over, refused to leave; and this was how the infidels started to enslave Greece. So anyone who does not want military success should have recourse to this kind of force, because it is far more dangerous than a mercenary army. Auxiliaries are fatal; they constitute a united army, wholly obedient to the orders of someone else; but mercenaries, having conquered, need more time and opportunity to harm you, for they are not a compact force and you have raised and paid them yourself. Mercenaries, also, are led by someone you appoint, and he cannot immediately assume sufficient authority to be able to do you harm. To sum up, cowardice is the danger with mercenaries, and valour with auxiliaries.

Wise princes, therefore, have always shunned auxiliaries and made use of their own forces. They have preferred to lose battles with their own forces than win them with others, in the belief that no true victory is possible with alien arms. Now, I shall never hesitate to cite Cesare Borgia and his conduct as an example. The duke used auxiliaries in his invasion of the Romagna, going there at the head of French troops. With those, he took Imola and Forlì. But then he decided that they were unsafe, and he turned to mercenaries in the belief that less risk was involved, hiring the Orsini and the Vitelli.

In making use of these, he found them to be suspect, disloyal, and dangerous; so he got rid of them and raised his own forces. And one can easily see the difference between these forces by considering the difference between the standing of the duke when he had only the French, when he had the Orsini and the Vitelli, and when he relied only on his own forces and himself. He grew in stature at each stage; and he was held in real respect only when everyone saw that he was absolute master of his armies.

I did not want to depart from recent, Italian examples, yet I do not want to ignore Hiero of Syracuse, one of those I mentioned before. As I said then, when the Syracusans had given him command of their armies he immediately realized that the mercenaries were useless; they were hired troops organized like our Italian mercenaries. It seemed to him impossible either to keep them or to disband them, so he had them all cut to pieces. And then he made war with his own, not with alien, soldiers. I would also like to recall to mind an allegory from the Old Testament, which is relevant to my argument. David offered Saul to go and fight Goliath, the Philistine champion, and Saul, to inspire him with courage, gave him his own weapons and armour. Having tried these on, David rejected them, saying that he would be unable to fight well with them and therefore he wanted to face the enemy with his sling and his knife. In short, armour belonging to someone else either drops off you or weighs you down or is too tight. When Charles VII, the father of King Louis XI, had by good fortune and prowess liberated France from the English, he realized the need to have his own armed forces, and set up the militia composed of mounted troops and infantry. Subsequently, his son King Louis abolished the ordinance governing the infantry and started to hire Swiss soldiers; and this mistake, followed by others, has as we can now see been the cause of the dangers threatening that kingdom. The increased standing allowed the Swiss has demoralized the rest of the army; the infantry have been abolished altogether, and the mounted troops have been made dependent on foreign troops, because being accustomed to take the field along with the Swiss they have come to believe that without them they cannot win a battle. Because of this, the French are no match for the Swiss, and without Swiss help feel no match for anyone else. So France has made use of a mixed force, partly mercenary and partly citizen: this combination is far better than a purely auxiliary or purely mercenary force, and far inferior to a citizen army. The example of France should be enough, because that kingdom would be unbeatable if what Charles had instituted had been developed or maintained. But men are so imprudent that they take up a diet which, as it tastes good to start with, they do not realize is poisonous, a point I made before, when talking about wasting fevers.

The prince who does not detect evils the moment they appear is lacking in true wisdom; but few rulers have the ability to do so. If we consider what was the start of the downfall of the Roman empire, it will be found that it was simply when the Goths started to be hired as mercenaries. To that small beginning can be traced the enervation of the forces of the Roman empire.

And the Goths inherited the prowess which the Romans lost.

I conclude, therefore, that unless it commands its own arms no principality is secure; rather, it is dependent on fortune, since there is no valour and no loyalty to defend it when adversity comes. Wise men have always held and believed: *'quod nihil sit tam infirmum aut instabile quam fama potentiae non sua vi nixa'.** One's own forces are composed of an army of one's subjects or an army of citizens or dependants; all other forces are either mercenaries or auxiliaries. It is easy to discover how to organize one's own forces if one studies the precedents set by the four rulers I named above, and if one understands how Philip, the father of Alexander the Great, and many other republics and princes, have armed and organized themselves: I willingly defer to the wisdom of what they instituted.

XIV
How a prince should organize his militia

A prince, therefore, must have no other object or thought, nor acquire skill in anything, except war, its organization, and its discipline. The art of war is all that is expected of a ruler; and it is so useful that besides enabling hereditary princes to maintain their rule it frequently enables ordinary citizens to become rulers. On

---

* 'That nothing is so weak or unstable as a reputation for power which is not based on one's own forces.'

the other hand, we find that princes who have thought more of their pleasures than of arms have lost their states. The first way to lose your state is to neglect the art of war; the first way to win a state is to be skilled in the art of war.

Francesco Sforza, because he was armed, from being an ordinary citizen rose to be duke of Milan; his sons, because they fled the hardships involved, sank to being ordinary citizens after being dukes. You are bound to meet misfortune if you are unarmed because, among other reasons, people despise you, and this, as I shall say later on, is one of the infamies a prince should be on his guard against. There is simply no comparison between a man who is armed and one who is not. It is unreasonable to expect that an armed man should obey one who is unarmed, or that an unarmed man should remain safe and secure when his servants are armed. In the latter case, there will be suspicion on the one hand and contempt on the other, making cooperation impossible. So a prince who does not understand warfare, as well as the other misfortunes he invites, cannot be respected by his soldiers or place any trust in them.

So he must never let his thoughts stray from military exercises, which he must pursue more vigorously in peace than in war. These exercises can be both physical and mental. As for the first, besides keeping his men well organized and trained, he must always be out hunting, so accustoming his body to hardships and also learning some practical geography: how the mountains slope, how the valleys open, how the plains spread out. He must study rivers and marshes; and in all this he should take great pains. Such knowledge is useful in two ways: first, if he obtains a clear understanding of local geography he will have a better understanding of how to organize his defence; and in addition his knowledge of and acquaintance with local conditions will make it easy for him to grasp the features of any new locality with which he may need to familiarize himself. For example, the hills and valleys, the plains, the rivers, and the marshes of Tuscany have certain features in common with those of other provinces; so with a knowledge of the geography of one particular province one can easily acquire knowledge of the geography of others. The prince who lacks this knowledge also lacks the first qualification of a good commander. This kind of ability teaches him how to locate the enemy, where to take up quarters, how to lead his army on the march and draw it up for battle, and lay siege to a town to the best advantage.

Philopoemen, the leader of the Achaeans, has been praised by the historians for, among other things, having never in peacetime thought of anything else except military strategy. When he was in the country with his friends, he would often stop and invite a discussion: if the enemy were on top of that hill, and we were down here with our army, which of us would have the advantage? How would one engage them without breaking ranks? If we wanted to retreat, how would we have to set about it? If they retreated, how would we best pursue them?

And, as they went along, he expounded to his friends all the contingencies that can befall an army; he heard their opinion, gave his own, and corroborated it with reasons. As a result, because of these continuous speculations, when he was leading his armies he knew how to cope with all and every emergency.

As for intellectual training, the prince must read history, studying the actions of eminent men to see how they conducted themselves during war and to discover the reasons for their victories or their defeats, so that he can avoid the latter and imitate the former. Above all, he must read history so that he can do what eminent men have done before him: taken as their model some historical figure who has been praised and honoured; and always kept his deeds and actions before them. In this way, it is said, Alexander the Great imitated Achilles; Caesar imitated Alexander; and Scipio, Cyrus. And anyone who reads the life of Cyrus, written by Xenophon, will then see how much of the glory won by Scipio can be attributed to his emulation of Cyrus, and how much, in his chastity, courtesy, humanity, and generosity, Scipio conformed to the picture which Xenophon drew of Cyrus.

A wise prince must observe these rules; he must never take things easy in times of peace, but rather use the latter assiduously, in order to be able to reap the profit in times of adversity. Then, when his fortunes change, he will be found ready to resist adversity.

XV

The things for which men, and especially princes, are praised or blamed

It now remains for us to see how a prince must regulate his conduct towards his subjects or his allies. I know that this has often been written about before, and so I hope it will not be thought presumptuous for me to do so, as, especially in discussing this subject, I draw up an original set of rules. But since my intention is to say something that will prove of practical use to the inquirer, I have thought it proper to represent things as they are in a real truth, rather than as they are imagined. Many have dreamed up republics and principalities which have never in truth been known to exist; the gulf between how one should live and how one does live is so wide that a man who neglects what is actually done for what should be done moves towards self-destruction rather than self-preservation. The fact is that a man who wants to act virtuously in every way necessarily comes to grief among so many who are not virtuous. Therefore if a prince wants to maintain his rule he must be prepared not to be virtuous, and to make use of this or not according to need.

So leaving aside imaginary things about a prince, and referring only to those which truly exist, I say that whenever men are discussed and especially princes (who are more exposed to view), they are judged for various qualities which earn them either praise or condemnation. Some, for example, are held to be generous, and others miserly (I use the Tuscan word rather than the word avaricious: we also call a man who is mean with what he possesses, miserly, whereas avaricious applies also to a man who wants to plunder others). Some are held to be benefactors, others are called grasping; some cruel, some compassionate; one man faithless, another faithful; one man effeminate and cowardly, another fierce and courageous; one man courteous, another proud; one man lascivious, another chaste; one guileless, another crafty; one stubborn, another flexible; one grave, another frivolous; one religious, another sceptical; and so forth. I know everyone will agree that it would be most laudable if a prince possessed all the qualities deemed to be good among those I have enumerated. But, because of conditions in the world, princes cannot have those qualities, or observe them completely. So a prince has of necessity to be so prudent that he knows how to escape the evil reputation attached to those vices which could lose him his state, and how to avoid those vices which are not so dangerous, if he possibly can; but, if he cannot, he need not worry so much about the latter. And then, he must not flinch from being blamed for vices which are necessary for safeguarding the state. This is because, taking everything into account, he will find that some of the things that appear to be virtues will, if he practises them, ruin him, and some of the things that appear to be vices will bring him security and prosperity.

XVI
Generosity and parsimony

So, starting with the first of the qualities I enumerated above, I say it would be splendid if one had a reputation for generosity; none the less if you do in fact earn a reputation for generosity you will come to grief. This is because if your generosity is good and sincere it may pass unnoticed and it will not save you from being reproached for its opposite. If you want to sustain a reputation for generosity, therefore, you have to be ostentatiously lavish; and a prince acting in that fashion will soon squander all his resources, only to be forced in the end, if he wants to maintain his reputation, to lay excessive burdens on the people, to impose extortionate taxes, and to do everything else he can to raise money. This will start to make his subjects hate him, and, since he will have impoverished himself, he will be generally despised. As a result, because of this generosity of his, having injured many and rewarded few, he will be vulnerable to the first minor setback, and the first real danger he encounters will bring him to grief. When he realizes this and tries to retrace his path he will immediately be reputed a miser.

So because a prince cannot practise the virtue of generosity in such a way that he is noted for it, except to his cost, he should if he is prudent not mind being called a miser. In time he will be recognized as being essentially a generous man, seeing that because of his parsimony his existing revenues are enough for him, he can defend himself against an aggressor, and he can embark on campaigns without burdening the people. So he proves himself generous to all those from whom he takes nothing, and they are innumerable, and miserly towards all those to whom he gives nothing, and they are few. In our own times great things have been accomplished only by those who have been held miserly, and the others have met disaster. Pope Julius II made use of a reputation for generosity to win the papacy but subsequently he made no effort to maintain this reputation, because he wanted to be able to finance his wars. The present king of France has been able to wage so many wars without taxing his subjects excessively only because his long-standing parsimony enabled him to meet the additional expenses involved. Were the present king of Spain renowned for his generosity he would not have started and successfully concluded so many enterprises.

So a prince must think little of it, if he incurs the name of miser, so as not to rob his subjects, to be able to defend himself, not to become poor and despicable, not to be forced to grow rapacious. Miserliness is one of those vices which sustain his rule. Someone may object: Caesar came to power by virtue of his generosity, and many others, because they practised and were known for their generosity, have risen to the very highest positions. My answer to this is as follows. Either you are already a prince, or you are on the way to becoming one. In the first case, your generosity will be to your cost; in the second, it is certainly necessary to have a reputation for generosity. Caesar was one of those who wanted to establish his own rule over Rome; but if, after he had established it, he had remained alive and not moderated his expenditure he would have fallen from power.

Again, someone may retort: there have been many princes who have won great successes with their armies, and who have had the reputation of being extremely generous. My reply to this is: the prince gives away what is his own or his subjects', or else what belongs to others. In the first case he should be frugal; in the second, he should indulge his generosity to the full. The prince who campaigns with his armies, who lives by pillaging, sacking, and extortion, disposes of what belongs to aliens; and he must be open-handed, otherwise the soldiers would refuse to follow him. And you can be more liberal with what does not belong to you or your subjects, as Caesar, Cyrus, and Alexander were. Giving away what belongs to strangers in no way affects your standing at home; rather it increases it. You hurt yourself only when you give away what is your own. There is nothing so self-defeating as generosity: in the act of practising it, you lose the ability to do so, and you become either poor and despised or, seeking to escape poverty, rapacious and hated. A prince must try to avoid, above all else, being despised and hated; and generosity results in your being both. Therefore it is wiser to incur the reputation of being a miser, which brings forth ignominy but not hatred, than to be forced by seeking a name for generosity to incur a reputation for rapacity, which brings you hatred as well as ignominy.

XVII
Cruelty and compassion; and whether it is better to be loved than feared, or the reverse

Taking others of the qualities I enumerated above, I say that a prince must want to have a reputation for compassion rather than for cruelty: none the less, he must be careful that he does not make bad use of compassion. Cesare Borgia was accounted cruel; nevertheless, this cruelty of his reformed the Romagna, brought it unity, and restored order and obedience. On reflection, it will be seen that there was more compassion in Cesare than in the Florentine people, who, to escape being called cruel, allowed Pistoia to be devastated. So a prince must not worry if he incurs reproach for his cruelty so long as he keeps his subjects united and loyal. By making an example or two he will prove more compassionate than those who, being too compassionate, allow disorders which lead to murder and rapine. These nearly always harm the whole community, whereas executions ordered by a prince only affect individuals. A new prince, of all rulers, finds it impossible to avoid a reputation for cruelty, because of the abundant dangers inherent in a newly won state. Vergil, through the mouth of Dido, says:

> Res dura, et regni novitas me talia cogunt
> Moliri, et late fines custode tueri.*

---

* 'Harsh necessity, and the newness of my kingdom, force me to do such things and to guard my frontiers everywhere.'

None the less, a prince must be slow to believe allegations and to take action, and must watch that he does not come to be afraid of his own shadow; his behaviour must be tempered by humanity and prudence so that over-confidence does not make him rash or excessive distrust make him unbearable.

From this arises the following question: whether it is better to be loved than feared, or the reverse. The answer is that one would like to be both the one and the other; but because it is difficult to combine them, it is far better to be feared than loved if you cannot be both. One can make this generalization about men: they are ungrateful, fickle, liars, and deceivers, they shun danger and are greedy for profit; while you treat them well, they are yours. They would shed their blood for you, risk their property, their lives, their sons, so long, as I said above, as danger is remote; but when you are in danger they turn away. Any prince who has come to depend entirely on promises and has taken no other precautions ensures his own ruin; friendship which is bought with money and not with greatness and nobility of mind is paid for, but it does not last and it yields nothing. Men worry less about doing an injury to one who makes himself loved than to one who makes himself feared. For love is secured by a bond of gratitude which men, wretched creatures that they are, break when it is to their advantage to do so; but fear is strengthened by a dread of punishment which is always effective.

The prince must none the less make himself feared in such a way that, if he is not loved, at least he escapes being hated. For fear is quite compatible with an absence of hatred; and the prince can always avoid hatred if he abstains from the property of his subjects and citizens and from their women. If, even so, it proves necessary to execute someone, this is to be done only when there is proper justification and manifest reason for it. But above all a prince must abstain from the property of others; because men sooner forget the death of their father than the loss of their patrimony. It is always possible to find pretexts for confiscating someone's property; and a prince who starts to live by rapine always finds pretexts for seizing what belongs to others. On the other hand, pretexts for executing someone are harder to find and they are sooner gone.

However, when a prince is campaigning with his soldiers and is in command of a large army then he need not worry about having a reputation for cruelty; because, without such a reputation, no army was ever kept united and disciplined. Among the admirable achievements of Hannibal is included this: that although he led a huge army, made up of countless different races, on foreign campaigns, there was never any dissension, either among the troops themselves or against their leader, whether things were going well or badly. For this, his inhuman cruelty was wholly responsible. It was this, along with his countless other qualities, which made him feared and respected by his soldiers. If it had not been for his cruelty, his other qualities would not have been enough. The historians, having given little thought to this, on the one hand admire what Hannibal achieved, and on the other condemn what made his achievements possible.

That his other qualities would not have been enough

by themselves can be proved by looking at Scipio, a man unique in his own time and through all recorded history. His armies mutinied against him in Spain, and the only reason for this was his excessive leniency, which allowed his soldiers more licence than was good for military discipline. Fabius Maximus reproached him for this in the Senate and called him a corrupter of the Roman legions. Again, when the Locrians were plundered by one of Scipio's officers, he neither gave them satisfaction nor punished his officer's insubordination; and this was all because of his being too lenient by nature. By way of excuse for him some senators argued that many men were better at not making mistakes themselves than at correcting them in others. But in time Scipio's lenient nature would have spoilt his fame and glory had he continued to indulge it during his command; when he lived under orders from the Senate, however, this fatal characteristic of his was not only concealed but even brought him glory.

So, on this question of being loved or feared, I conclude that since some men love as they please but fear when the prince pleases, a wise prince should rely on what he controls, not on what he cannot control. He must only endeavour, as I said, to escape being hated.

XVIII
How princes should honour their word

Everyone realizes how praiseworthy it is for a prince to honour his word and to be straightforward rather than crafty in his dealings; none the less contemporary experience shows that princes who have achieved great things have been those who have given their word lightly, who have known how to trick men with their cunning, and who, in the end, have overcome those abiding by honest principles.

You must understand, therefore, that there are two ways of fighting: by law or by force. The first way is natural to men, and the second to beasts. But as the first way often proves inadequate one must needs have recourse to the second. So a prince must understand how to make a nice use of the beast and the man. The ancient writers taught princes about this by an allegory, when they described how Achilles and many other princes of the ancient world were sent to be brought up by Chiron, the centaur, so that he might train them his way. All the allegory means, in making the teacher half beast and half man, is that a prince must know how to act according to the nature of both, and that he cannot survive otherwise.

So, as a prince is forced to know how to act like a beast, he must learn from the fox and the lion; because the lion is defenceless against traps and a fox is defenceless against wolves. Therefore one must be a fox in order to recognize traps, and a lion to frighten off wolves. Those who simply act like lions are stupid. So it follows that a prudent ruler cannot, and must not, honour his word when it places him at a disadvantage and when the reasons for which he made his promise no longer exist. If all men were good, this precept would not be good; but because men are wretched creatures who would not keep their word to you, you need not keep your word to them. And no prince ever lacked good excuses to colour his bad faith. One could give innumerable modern instances of this, showing how many pacts and promises have been made null and void by the bad faith of princes: those who have known best how to imitate the fox have come off best. But one must know how to colour one's actions and to be a great liar and deceiver. Men are so simple, and so much creatures of circumstance, that the deceiver will always find someone ready to be deceived.

There is one fresh example I do not want to omit. Alexander VI never did anything, or thought of anything, other than deceiving men; and he always found victims for his deceptions. There never was a man capable of such convincing asseverations, or so ready to swear to the truth of something, who would honour his word less. None the less his deceptions always had the result he intended, because he was a past master in the art.

A prince, therefore, need not necessarily have all the good qualities I mentioned above, but he should certainly appear to have them. I would even go so far as to say that if he has these qualities and always behaves accordingly he will find them harmful; if he only appears to have them they will render him service. He should appear to be compassionate, faithful to his word, kind, guileless and devout. And indeed he should be so. But his disposition should be such that, if he needs to be the opposite, he knows how. You must realize this: that a prince, and especially a new prince, cannot observe all those things which give men a reputation for virtue, because in order to maintain his state he is often forced to act in defiance of good faith, of charity, of kindness, of religion. And so he should have a flexible disposition, varying as fortune and circumstances dictate. As I said above, he should not deviate from what is good, if that is possible, but he should know how to do evil, if that is necessary.

A prince, then, must be very careful not to say a word which does not seem inspired by the five qualities I mentioned earlier. To those seeing and hearing him, he should appear a man of compassion, a man of good faith, a man of integrity, a kind and a religious man. And there is nothing so important as to seem to have this last quality. Men in general judge by their eyes rather than by their hands; because everyone is in a position to watch, few are in a position to come in close touch with you. Everyone sees what you appear to be, few experience what you really are. And those few dare not gainsay the many who are backed by the majesty of the state. In the actions of all men, and especially of princes, where there is no court of appeal, one judges by the result. So let a prince set about the task of conquering, and maintaining his state; his methods will always be judged honourable and will be universally praised. The common people are always impressed by appearances and results. In this context, there are only common people, and there is no leeway for the few when the many are firmly sustained. A certain contemporary ruler, whom it is better not to name, never preaches anything except peace and good faith; and he is an enemy of both one and the other, and if he had ever honoured either of them he would have lost either his standing or his state many times over.

XIX
The need to avoid contempt and hatred

Now, having talked about the most important of the qualities enumerated above, I want to discuss the others briefly under this generalization: that the prince should, as I have already suggested, determine to avoid anything which will make him hated and despised. So long as he does so, he will have done what he should and he will run no risk whatsoever if he is reproached for the other vices I mentioned. He will be hated above all if, as I said, he is rapacious and aggressive with regard to the property and the women of his subjects. He must refrain from these. As long as he does not rob the great majority of their property or their honour, they remain content. He then has to contend only with the ambition of a few, and that can be dealt with easily and in a variety of ways. He will be despised if he has a reputation for being fickle, frivolous, effeminate, cowardly, irresolute; a prince should avoid this like the plague and strive to demonstrate in his actions grandeur, courage, sobriety, strength. When settling disputes between his subjects, he should ensure that his judgement is irrevocable; and he should be so regarded that no one ever dreams of trying to deceive or trick him.

The prince who succeeds in having himself thus regarded is highly esteemed; and against a man who is highly esteemed conspiracy is difficult, and open attack is difficult, provided he is recognized as a great man, who is respected by his subjects. There are two things a prince must fear: internal subversion from his subjects; and external aggression by foreign powers. Against the latter, his defence lies in being well armed and having good allies; and if he is well armed he will always have good allies. In addition, domestic affairs will always remain under control provided that relations with external powers are under control and if indeed they were not disturbed by a conspiracy. Even if there is disturbance abroad, if the prince has ordered his government and lived as I said, and if he does not capitulate, he will always repulse every onslaught, just as I said Nabis the Spartan did. Now, as far as his subjects are concerned, when there is no disturbance abroad the prince's chief fear must be a secret conspiracy. He can adequately guard against this if he avoids being hated or scorned and keeps the people satisfied: this, as I have said above at length, is crucial. One of the most powerful safeguards a prince can have against conspiracies is to avoid being hated by the populace. This is because the conspirator always thinks that by killing the prince he will satisfy the people; but if he thinks that he will outrage the people, he will never have the courage to go ahead with his enterprise, because there are countless obstacles in the path of a conspirator. As experience shows, there have been many conspiracies but few of them have achieved their end. This is because the conspirator needs others to help him, and those have to be men who, he believes, are disgruntled. But as soon as he reveals his mind to a man who is dissatisfied he gives him the means to get satisfaction, because by telling all he knows the latter can hope to obtain all he wants. Seeing the sure profit to be won by informing, and the highly dangerous and doubtful alternative, a man must be either a rare friend indeed or else an utterly relentless enemy of the prince to keep faith with you. To put it briefly, I say that on the side of the conspirator there is nothing except fear, envy, and the terrifying prospect of punishment; on the side of the prince there is the majesty of government, there are laws, the resources of his friends and of the state to protect him. Add to all these the goodwill of the people, and it is unthinkable that anyone should be so rash as to conspire. For whereas in the normal course of events a conspirator has cause for fear before he acts, in this case he has cause for fear afterwards as well, seeing that the people are hostile to him. He will have accomplished his crime, and, because the people are against him, he will have no place of refuge.

I could give countless illustrations of this; but I will content myself with just one, which happened in the time of our fathers. The Canneschi conspired against and killed messer Annibale Bentivogli, grandfather of the present Annibale, and prince of Bologna. There remained as his heir only messer Giovanni, who was still in swaddling clothes. Immediately this murder was perpetrated, the people rose up and killed all the Canneschi. They were inspired by the goodwill that existed for the House of Bentivoglio at that period. It was so great that, although there was no member of the family left in Bologna to take over the government on the death of

Annibale, the citizens of Bologna, hearing that there was someone in Florence who was of the Bentivoglio family but had until then been thought to be the son of a smith, went there to find him. They entrusted him with the government of the city; and he ruled until Giovanni was old enough to assume the government himself.

I conclude, therefore, that when a prince has the goodwill of the people he must not worry about conspiracies; but when the people are hostile and regard him with hatred he must go in fear of everything and everyone. Well-organized states and wise princes have always taken great pains not to make the nobles despair, and to satisfy the people and keep them content; this is one of the most important tasks a prince must undertake.

Among kingdoms which are well organized and governed, in our own time, is that of France: it possesses countless valuable institutions, on which the king's freedom of action and security depend. The first of these is the parliament and its authority. For the lawgiver of the French kingdom, knowing the ambition and insolence of the powerful, judged it necessary that they should be restrained by having a bit in their mouths. On the other hand, he wanted to protect the masses, knowing how they feared, and therefore hated, the nobles. He did not want this to be the particular responsibility of the king, because he wished to save him from being reproached by the nobles for favouring the people and by the people for favouring the nobles. So he instituted an independent arbiter to crush the nobles and favour the weak, without bringing reproach on the king. There could be no better or more sensible institution, nor one more effective in ensuring the security of the king and the kingdom.

From this can be drawn another noteworthy consideration: that princes should delegate to others the enactment of unpopular measures and keep in their own hands the means of winning favours. Again, I conclude that a prince should value the nobles, but not make himself hated by the people.

Many who have studied the lives and deaths of certain Roman emperors may perhaps believe that they provide examples contradicting my opinion; some emperors who led consistently worthy lives, and showed strength of character, none the less fell from power, or were even done to death by their own men who conspired against them. As I wish to answer these objections, I shall discuss the characters of some of the emperors, showing that the reasons for their downfall are not different from those I have adduced. I shall submit for consideration examples which are well known to students of the period. I shall also restrict myself to all those emperors who came to power from Marcus the philosopher to Maximinus. These were: Marcus Aurelius, Commodus his son, Pertinax, Julian, Severus, Caracalla his son, Macrinus, Heliogabalus, Alexander, and Maximinus.

First, it is to be noted that whereas other princes have to contend only with the ambition of the nobles and the insolence of the people, the Roman emperors encountered a third difficulty: they had to contend with the cruelty and avarice of the soldiers. This was a hard task and it was responsible for the downfall of many, since it was difficult to satisfy both the soldiers and the populace.

The latter, being peace-loving, liked unadventurous emperors, while the soldiers loved a warlike ruler, and one who was arrogant, cruel, and rapacious. They wanted him to treat the people accordingly, so that they could be paid more and could give vent to their own avarice and cruelty. As a result, those emperors who did not have the natural authority or the standing to hold both the soldiers and the populace in check always came to grief. Most of them, especially those who were new to government, when they recognized the difficulty of satisfying these two diverse elements, appeased the soldiers and did not worry about injuring the populace. This policy was necessary: princes cannot help arousing hatred in some quarters, so first they must strive not to be hated by all and every class of subject; and when this proves impossible, they should strive assiduously to escape the hatred of the most powerful classes. Therefore those emperors who, because they were new men, needed out of the ordinary support, were more ready to throw in their lot with the soldiers than with the people. None the less, this proved to be advantageous or not depending on whether the ruler knew how to maintain his standing with the troops. Now, for the reasons given above, it came about that Marcus Aurelius, Pertinax, and Alexander, who all lived unadventurously, who loved justice, hated cruelty, were kind and courteous, all, Marcus apart, had an unhappy end. Marcus alone was held during his life and after in high esteem, because he succeeded to the empire by hereditary right, and did not have to thank either the soldiers or the populace for it. Then, as he possessed many qualities which earned him great respect, all his life he succeeded in holding both of these in check and he was never hated or scorned. But Pertinax came to grief in the early stages of his administration; he was created emperor against the will of the soldiers, who had been used to living licentiously under Commodus and so could not tolerate the decency which Pertinax wished to impose on them. So the emperor made himself hated, and also, since he was an old man, scorned.

And here it should be noted that one can be hated just as much for good deeds as for evil ones; therefore, as I said above, a prince who wants to maintain his rule is often forced not to be good, because whenever that class of men on which you believe your continued rule depends is corrupt, whether it be the populace, or soldiers, or nobles, you have to satisfy it by adopting the same disposition; and then good deeds are your enemies. But let us come to Alexander. He was a man of such goodness that, among the other things for which he is given credit, it is said that during the fourteen years he reigned he never put anyone to death without trial. None the less, as he was thought effeminate, and a man who let himself be ruled by his mother, he came to be scorned, and the army conspired against him and killed him.

Discussing in contrast the characters of Commodus, Severus, Antonius Caracalla, and Maximinus, you will find them to have been extremely cruel and rapacious. To satisfy the soldiers, there was no kind of injury they did not inflict on the people; and all of them, except Severus, came to an unhappy end. Severus was a man of such prowess that, keeping the soldiers friendly, even though the people were oppressed by him, he reigned successfully to the end; this was because his prowess so impressed the soldiers and the people that the latter were in a certain manner left astonished and stupefied and the former stayed respectful and content.

Because what Severus did was remarkable and outstanding for a new prince, I want to show briefly how well he knew how to act the part of both a fox and a lion, whose natures, as I say above, must be imitated by a new prince. Knowing the indolence of the emperor Julian, Severus persuaded the troops he commanded in Slavonia to march on Rome to avenge the death of Pertinax, who had been put to death by the Praetorian Guards. Under this pretext, without any indication that he aspired to the empire, he moved the army against Rome; and he arrived in Italy before it was known that he had set out. When he came, the Senate, out of fear, elected him emperor and put Julian to death. After this start, there remained two obstacles in the way of his becoming master of all the state: one was in Asia, where Pescennius Niger, commander of the Asiatic army, had had himself proclaimed emperor; the other was in the west, where Albinus also aspired to the empire. Judging it was dangerous to show himself hostile to both of them, Severus decided to attack Niger and to trick Albinus. He wrote to the latter saying that, having been elected emperor by the Senate, he wished to share the high rank with him; he sent him the title of Caesar and, through a resolution in the Senate, he made him co-emperor. Albinus took all these things at their face value. But once

Severus had defeated Niger and put him to death, and had pacified the East, he returned to Rome and complained in the Senate that Albinus, not recognizing the favours he had received from him, had treacherously sought to kill him. Because of this, Severus added, it was necessary for him to go and punish such ingratitude. He then marched against him in France, and took from him his state and his life.

So whoever carefully studies what this man did will find that he had the qualities of a ferocious lion and a very cunning fox, and that he was feared and respected by everyone, yet not hated by the troops. And it will not be thought anything to marvel at if Severus, an upstart, proved himself able to maintain such great power; because his tremendous prestige always protected him from the hatred which his plundering had inspired in the people. Now Antoninus Caracalla, his son, was also a man of splendid qualities which astonished the people and endeared him to the soldiers; he was a military man, capable of any exertion, and he scorned softness of any kind, at the table or elsewhere. This won him the devotion of the troops. None the less, his ferocity and cruelty were so great and unparalleled (after countless individual murders, he put to death great numbers of Romans and all the citizens of Alexandria) that he became universally hated. Even those closest to him started to fear him; and as a result he was killed by a centurion, when he was surrounded by his troops. Here it should be noted that princes cannot escape death if the attempt is made by a fanatic, because anyone who has no fear of death himself can succeed in inflicting it; on the other hand, there is less need for a prince to be afraid, since such assassinations are very rare. However, the prince should restrain himself from inflicting grave injury on anyone in his service whom he has close to him in his affairs of state. That was how Antoninus erred. He put to death, with disgrace, a brother of that centurion, whom in turn he threatened every day even though still retaining him in his bodyguard. This rash behaviour was calculated to bring him grief, as in the end it did.

But let us come to Commodus, for whom ruling the empire was an easy task, since being the son of Marcus Aurelius he held it by hereditary right. He had only to follow in the footsteps of his father, and then he would have satisfied the soldiers and the people. But, as he was of a cruel, bestial disposition, he endeavoured to indulge the soldiers and make them dissolute, in order to exercise his rapacity on the people. On the other hand, he forgot his dignity, often descended into the amphitheatres to fight with the gladiators, and did other ignoble things hardly worthy of the imperial majesty; as a result the soldiers came to despise him. So, being hated on the one side and scorned on the other, he fell victim to a conspiracy which ended in his death.

It now remains for us to describe the character of Maximinus. He was a very warlike man, and the troops, being sick of the effeminacies of Alexander, whom I discussed above, elected him emperor after Alexander's death. He did not hold the empire for long, because two things made him hated and despised: first, he was of the lowest origins, having once been a shepherd in Thrace (this was well known to everybody and lowered him in everyone's eyes); second, at his accession he put off going to Rome to be formally hailed as emperor, and he impressed people as being extremely savage because he inflicted many cruelties through his prefects in Rome and in other parts of the empire. As a result, there was a universal upsurge of indignation against him because of his mean birth, and an upsurge of hatred caused by fear of his ferocity. First Africa rebelled, and then the Senate with the support of all the people of Rome. All Italy conspired against him. The conspiracy was joined by his own troops who, when they were besieging Aquileia and finding difficulties in taking the town, sickened of his cruelty; seeing how many enemies he had they feared him less, and they killed him.

I do not want to discuss Heliogabalus, or Macrinus, or Julian, who were thoroughly despised and therefore did not last long. Instead I shall conclude by saying that contemporary princes are less troubled by this problem of having to take extraordinary measures to satisfy the soldiers. They do have to give them some consideration; but notwithstanding this the problem is soon settled, because princes today do not possess standing armies which, like the armies of the Roman Empire, have become firmly established in the government and administration of conquered territories. So if in Roman times it was necessary to satisfy the demands of the soldiers rather than those of the people, this was because the soldiers had more power than the people. In our own times it is necessary for all rulers, except the Turk and the Sultan, to conciliate the people rather than the soldiers, because the people are the more powerful. I make an exception of the Turk, because that ruler maintains a standing army of twelve thousand infantry and fifteen thousand cavalry, essential to the security and strength of his kingdom; and so he must subordinate every other consideration to that of retaining their loyalty. Similarly, the Sultan's dominion is completely in the hands of his soldiers, and he also, without regard for the people, must make sure of their allegiance to him. You should note that the Sultan's state differs from all the other principalities, being similar to the papacy, which cannot be called either a hereditary or a new principality. It is not the sons of the former ruler who inherit and become rulers but the one elected by those with the authority to do so. As this system is an ancient one it cannot be classified among the new principalities. There are none of the difficulties encountered in a new principality; although the prince is new, the institutions of the state are old, and they are devised to accommodate him as if he were the hereditary ruler.

But let us go back to the subject. I say that whoever follows my argument will realize that the downfall of the emperors I mentioned was caused by either hatred or scorn. He will also recognize why it happened that, some of them behaving one way and some of them another, in both cases one ended happily and the rest came to grief. As they were new princes, it was useless and disastrous for Pertinax and Alexander to want to imitate Marcus Aurelius, who succeeded by hereditary right; similarly it was fatal for Caracalla, Commodus, and Maximinus to imitate Severus, since they lacked the prowess to follow in his footsteps. Therefore, a new prince in a new principality cannot imitate the actions of Marcus Aurelius, nor is he bound to follow those of Severus. Rather, he should select from Severus the qualities necessary to establish his state, and from Marcus Aurelius those which are conducive to its maintenance and glory after it has been stabilized and made secure.

XX

Whether fortresses and many of the other present-day expedients to which princes have recourse are useful or not

To keep a secure hold on their states some princes have disarmed their subjects; some have kept the towns subject to them divided; some have purposely fostered animosity against themselves; some have endeavoured to win over those who were initially suspect; some have put up fortresses; some have razed them to the ground. It is impossible to give a final verdict on any of these policies, unless one examines the particular circumstances of the states in which such decisions have had to be taken. None the less, I shall as far as possible discuss the matter in generalizations.

Now, no new prince has ever at any time disarmed his subjects; rather, when he has found them unarmed he has always given them arms. This is because by arming your subjects you arm yourself; those who were suspect become loyal, and those who were loyal not only remain so but are changed from being merely your subjects to being your partisans. Then, as it is impossible to arm everybody, when you have given this privilege to some you can deal more severely with the others. And this discrimination will, when it is understood, put the former under more of an obligation; the others will excuse you, judging that it is necessary for those who run more risks and incur greater obligations to be treated more favourably. But as soon as you disarm your subjects you start to offend them, showing whether through cowardice or suspicion that you mistrust them; and on either score hatred is aroused against you.

Then, since you cannot stay unarmed, you are forced to have recourse to mercenary troops, whose character is as I described above. And even if these mercenaries were reliable, they could not be sufficiently so to protect you against powerful enemies and against subjects you distrust. So, as I said, a new prince in a new principality always arms his subjects; and history is full of examples of this.

But when a prince acquires a state which is annexed to his original principality, like a new limb, then he must disarm his new subjects, except for those who were his partisans. Even they, as time and opportunity allow, must be made weak and effeminate, and matters must be so arranged that throughout your dominions only your own soldiers, serving near you in your original dominion, are armed.

Our ancestors, and those who were considered to be wise, were accustomed to say that it was necessary to control Pistoia by means of factions and Pisa by means of fortresses; so they fostered strife in various of their subject towns, so as to control them more easily. In those days when there was stability of a sort in Italy, this was doubtless sensible; but I do not think it makes a good rule today. I do not believe that any good at all ever comes of dissension. On the contrary, on the approach of the enemy, cities which are so divided inevitably succumb at once; the weaker faction will always go over to the invader, and the other will not be able to hold out.

The Venetians, influenced I believe by the considerations I gave above, fostered the Guelf and Ghibelline factions in their subject cities. Although they never allowed bloodshed, yet they fostered these discords so that the citizens, taken up with their own dissensions, might never combine against them. But, as we have seen, this did not turn out as they had planned, because when the Venetians were routed at Vailà one faction immediately summoned up courage and took the whole state from them. Such methods, therefore, argue for weakness on the part of the prince. In a strong principality such dissensions are never allowed. They profit the prince only in times of peace, when he can make use of them to handle his subjects more easily; but when war comes the weakness of this policy is revealed.

There is no doubt that a prince's greatness depends on his triumphing over difficulties and opposition. So fortune, especially when she wants to build up the greatness of a new prince, whose need to acquire standing is more pressing than that of a hereditary ruler, finds enemies for him and encourages them to take the field against him, so that he may have cause to triumph over them and ascend higher on the ladder his foes have provided. Many, therefore, believe that when he has the chance an able prince should cunningly foster some opposition to himself so that by overcoming it he can enhance his own stature.

Princes, especially new ones, have found men who were suspect at the start of their rule more loyal and more useful than those who, at the start, were their trusted friends. Pandolfo Petrucci, ruler of Siena, governed his state more with the support of those who had been suspect than with that of the others. But here generalization is impossible, because circumstances vary. I shall say just this: a prince will never have any difficulty in winning over those who were initially his enemies, when they are such that they need someone to lean upon. And they are all the more forced to serve him loyally inasmuch as they realize that it is more necessary for them to wipe out with their actions the bad opinion he had formed of them; and so the prince finds them more useful than those who feel themselves so secure in his service that they neglect his interests.

Since it is relevant to the subject, I shall remind princes who have recently seized a state for themselves through support given from within that they should carefully reflect on the motives of those who helped them. If these were not based on a natural affection for the new prince, but rather on discontent with the existing government, he will retain their friendship only with considerable difficulty and exertion, because it will be impossible for him in his turn to satisfy them. If we carefully examine the reasons for this, with examples taken from ancient and modern times, it will be found that a prince far more easily wins the friendship of those who were formerly satisfied with the existing government, and so were hostile to him then, than of those who, because they were dissatisfied, became his friends and favoured his occupation.

Princes, in order to hold their dominions more securely, have been accustomed to build fortresses, which act as a curb on those who may plot rebellion against them, and which provide a safe refuge from sudden attack. I approve of this policy, because it has been used from the time of the ancient world. None the less, in our own time, messer Niccolò Vitelli saw fit to raze two fortresses in Città di Castello, in order to maintain his hold there. Guidobaldo, duke of Urbino, after he returned to the dominion from which Cesare Borgia had chased him, razed to the ground all the fortresses in his province, in the belief that by doing so it would be more difficult for him to lose the state again; when they returned to Bologna, the Bentivoglio followed a similar policy. So we see that fortresses are useful or not depending on circumstances; and if they are beneficial in one direction, they are harmful in another. It can be put like this: the prince who is more afraid of his own people than of foreign interference should build fortresses; but the prince who fears foreign interference more than his own people should forget about them. The castle of Milan, built by Francesco Sforza, has caused and will cause more uprisings against the House of Sforza than any other source of disturbance. So the best fortress that exists is to avoid being hated by the people. If you have fortresses and yet the people hate you they will not save you; once the people have taken up arms they will never lack outside help. In our own time, there is no instance of a fortress proving its worth to any ruler, except in the case of the countess of Forlì, after her consort, count Girolamo, had been killed. In her case the fortress gave her a refuge against the assault of the populace, where she could wait for succour from Milan and then recover the state. Circumstances were such that the people could not obtain support from outside. But subsequently fortresses proved of little worth even to her, when Cesare Borgia attacked her and then her hostile subjects joined forces with the invader. So then as before it would have been safer for her to have avoided the enmity of the people than to have had fortresses. So, all things considered, I commend those who erect fortresses and those who do not; and I censure anyone who, putting his trust in fortresses, does not mind if he is hated by the people.

XXI
How a prince must act to win honour

Nothing brings a prince more prestige than great campaigns and striking demonstrations of his personal abilities. In our own time we have Ferdinand of Aragon, the present king of Spain. He can be regarded as a new prince, because from being a weak king he has risen to being, for fame and glory, the first king of Christendom. If you study his achievements, you will find that they were all magnificent and some of them unparalleled. At the start of his reign he attacked Granada; and this campaign laid the foundation of his power. First, he embarked on it undistracted, and without fear of interference; he used it to engage the energies of the barons of Castile who, as they were giving their minds to the war, had no mind for causing trouble at home. In this way, without their realizing what was happening, he increased his standing and his control over them. He was able to sustain his armies with money from the Church and the people, and, by means of that long war, to lay a good foundation for his standing army, which has subsequently won him renown. In addition, in order to be able to undertake even greater campaigns, still making use of religion, he turned his hand to a pious work of cruelty when he chased out the Moriscos and rid his kingdom of them; there could not have been a more pitiful or striking enterprise. Under the same cloak of religion he assaulted Africa; he started his campaign in Italy; he has recently attacked France. Thus he has always planned and completed great projects, which have always kept his subjects in a state of suspense and wonder, and intent on their outcome. And his moves have followed closely upon one another in such a way that he has never allowed time and opportunity in between times for people to foster conspiracies against him.

It is also very profitable for a prince to give striking demonstrations of his capabilities in regard to government at home, similar to those which are attributed to messer Bernabò of Milan; in the event that someone accomplishes something exceptional, for good or evil, in civil life, he should be rewarded or punished in a way that sets everyone talking. Above all, in all his doings a prince must endeavour to win the reputation of being a great man of outstanding ability.

A prince also wins prestige for being a true friend or a true enemy, that is, for revealing himself without any reservation in favour of one side against another. This policy is always more advantageous than neutrality. For instance, if the powers neighbouring on you come to blows, either they are such that, if one of them conquers, you will be in danger, or they are not. In either case it will always be to your advantage to declare yourself and to wage a vigorous war; because, in the first case, if you do not declare yourself you will always be at the mercy of the conqueror, much to the pleasure and satisfaction of the one who has been beaten, and you will have no justification nor any way to obtain protection or refuge. The conqueror does not want doubtful friends who do not help him when he is in difficulties; the loser repudiates you because you were unwilling to go, arms in hand, and throw in your lot with him.

Antiochus went into Greece, at the invitation of the Aetolians, to drive out the Romans. He sent envoys to the Achaeans, who were friends of the Romans, to encourage them to stand aside; for their part, the Romans started persuading the Achaeans to fight with them. The matter came to be debated in the council of the Achaeans, where the ambassador of Antiochus was urging them to remain neutral. To this, the Roman legate replied: '*Quod autem isti dicunt non interponendi vos bello, nihil magis alienum rebus vestris est; sine gratia, sine dignitate, praemium victoris eritis.*'*

* 'Nothing is more contrary to your interests than their advice, that you should not intervene in the war; you will become the prize of the victor, without favour or dignity.'

It is always the case that the one who is not your friend will request your neutrality, and that the one who is your friend will request your armed support. Princes who are irresolute usually follow the path of neutrality in order to escape immediate danger, and usually they come to grief. But when you boldly declare your support for one side, then if that side conquers, even though the victor is powerful and you are at his mercy, he is under an obligation to you and he has committed himself to friendly ties with you; and men are never so unprincipled as to deal harshly and ungratefully with you in this instance. Then again, victories are never so overwhelming that the conqueror does not have to show some scruples, especially regarding justice. If on the other hand your ally is defeated, he will shelter you; he will help you while he can, and you become associates whose joint fortunes may well change for the better. Now, in the second case, when the combatants are such that you need have no fear of the victor, there is all the more reason to support one side or the other. In this way you help destroy one combatant with the help of the other, who would be helping him himself if he were wise. If you are the victors, your ally is at your mercy, and with your help it is impossible for him not to win.

Here it is to be noted that a prince should never join in an aggressive alliance with someone more powerful than himself, unless it is a matter of necessity, as I said above. This is because if you are the victors, you emerge as his prisoner; and princes should do their utmost to escape being at the mercy of others. The Venetians joined with France against the duke of Milan, and they could have escaped making this alliance, which proved their undoing. But when such an alliance cannot be avoided (as was the case with the Florentines when the pope and Spain led their armies against Lombardy) then the prince should support one side or another for the reasons given above. Then, no government should ever imagine that it can always adopt a safe course; rather, it should regard all possible courses of action as risky. This is the way things are: whenever one tries to escape one danger one runs into another. Prudence consists in being able to assess the nature of a particular threat and in accepting the lesser evil.

A prince should also show his esteem for talent, actively encouraging able men, and honouring those who excel in their profession. Then he must encourage his citizens so that they can go peaceably about their business, whether it be trade or agriculture or any other human occupation. One man should not be afraid of improving his possessions, lest they be taken away from him, or another deterred by high taxes from starting a new business. Rather, the prince should be ready to reward men who want to do these things and anyone who endeavours in any way to increase the prosperity of his city or his state. As well as this, at suitable times of the year he should entertain the people with shows and festivities. And since every city is divided into guilds or family groups, he should pay attention to these, meet them from time to time, and give an example of courtesy and munificence, while all the time, none the less, fully maintaining the dignity of his position, because this should never be wanting in anything.

XXII
A prince's personal staff

The choosing of ministers is a matter of no little importance for a prince; and their worth depends on the sagacity of the prince himself. The first opinion that is formed of a ruler's intelligence is based on the quality of the men he has around him. When they are competent and loyal he can always be considered wise, because he has been able to recognize their competence and to keep them loyal. But when they are otherwise, the prince is always open to adverse criticism; because his first mistake has been in the choice of his ministers.

No one who knew messer Antonio da Venafro as the minister of Pandolfo Petrucci, prince of Siena, could but conclude that therefore Pandolfo was himself a man of great ability. There are three kinds of intelligence: one kind understands things for itself, the second appreciates what others can understand, the third understands neither for itself nor through others. This first kind is excellent, the second good, and the third kind useless. So it follows that Pandolfo, if he did not have the first kind of intelligence, at least had the second. If a prince has the discernment to recognize the good or bad in what another says or does, even though he has no acumen himself, he can see when his minister's actions are good or bad, and he can praise or correct accordingly; in this way, the minister cannot hope to deceive him and so takes care not to go wrong.

But as for how a prince can assess his minister, here

is an infallible guide: when you see a minister thinking more of himself than of you, and seeking his own profit in everything he does, such a one will never be a good minister, you will never be able to trust him. This is because a man entrusted with the task of government must never think of himself but of the prince, and must never concern himself with anything except the prince's affairs. To keep his minister up to the mark the prince, on his side, must be considerate towards him, must pay him honour, enrich him, put him in his debt, share with him both honours and responsibilities. Thus the minister will see how dependent he is on the prince; and then having riches and honours to the point of surfeit he will desire no more; holding so many offices, he cannot but fear changes. When, therefore, relations between princes and their ministers are of this kind, they can have confidence in each other; when they are otherwise, the result is always disastrous for one or the other of them.

XXIII
How flatterers must be shunned

There is one important subject I do not want to pass over, the mistake which princes can only with difficulty avoid making if they are not extremely prudent or do not choose their ministers well. I am referring to flatterers, who swarm in the courts. Men are so happily absorbed in their own affairs and indulge in such self-deception that it is difficult for them not to fall victim to this plague; and some efforts to protect oneself from flatterers involve the risk of becoming despised. This is because the only way to safeguard yourself against flatterers is by letting people understand that you are not offended by the truth; but if everyone can speak the truth to you then you lose respect. So a shrewd prince should adopt a middle way, choosing wise men for his government and allowing only those the freedom to speak the truth to him, and then only concerning matters on which he asks their opinion, and nothing else. But he should also question them thoroughly and listen to what they say; then he should make up his own mind, by himself. And his attitude towards his councils and towards each one of his advisers should be such that they will recognize that the more freely they speak out the more acceptable they will be. Apart from these, the prince should heed no one; he should put the policy agreed upon into effect straight away, and he should adhere to it rigidly. Anyone who does not do this is ruined by flatterers or is constantly changing his mind because of conflicting advice: as a result he is held in low esteem.

I want to give a modern illustration of this argument. Bishop Luca, in the service of Maximilian the present emperor, said of his majesty that he never consulted anybody and never did things as he wanted to; this happened because he did the opposite of what I said above. The emperor is a secretive man, he does not tell anyone of his plans, and he accepts no advice. But as soon as he puts his plans into effect, and they come to be known, they meet with opposition from those around him; and then he is only too easily diverted from his purpose. The result is that whatever he does one day is undone the next, what he wants or plans to do is never clear, and no reliance can be placed on his decisions.

A prince must, therefore, never lack advice. But he must take it when he wants to, not when others want him to; indeed, he must discourage everyone from tendering advice about anything unless it is asked for. All the same, he should be a constant questioner, and he must listen patiently to the truth regarding what he has inquired about. Moreover, if he finds that anyone for some reason holds the truth back he must show his wrath. And though many suppose that a prince may rightly be esteemed shrewd not because he is so himself but because of the quality of those there to advise him, they are undoubtedly mistaken. For this is an infallible rule: a prince who is not himself wise cannot be well advised, unless he happens to put himself in the hands of one individual who looks after all his affairs and is an extremely shrewd man. In this case, he may well be given good advice, but he would not last long because the man who governs for him would soon deprive him of his state. But when seeking advice of more than one person a prince who is not himself wise will never get unanimity in his councils or be able to reconcile their views. Each councillor will consult his own interests; and the prince will not know how to correct or understand them. Things cannot be otherwise, since men will always do badly by you unless they are forced to be virtuous. So the conclusion is that good advice, whomever it comes from, depends on the shrewdness of the prince who seeks it, and not the shrewdness of the prince on good advice.

XXIV
Why the Italian princes have lost their states

If he carefully observes the rules I have given above, a new prince will appear to have been long established and will quickly become more safe and secure in his government than if he had been ruling his state for a long time. The actions of a new prince attract much more attention than those of a hereditary ruler; and when these actions are marked by prowess they, far more than royal blood, win men over and capture their allegiance. This is because men are won over by the present far more than by the past; and when they decide that what is being done here and now is good, they content themselves with that and do not go looking for anything else. Indeed in that case they would do anything to defend their prince, provided he himself is not deficient in other things. Thus the new prince will have a twofold glory, in having founded a new state and in having adorned and strengthened it with good laws, sound defences, reliable allies, and inspiring leadership, just as the one who is born a prince and loses his state through incompetence is shamed twice over.

Let us consider those Italian rulers, such as the king of Naples, the duke of Milan, and so forth who have lost their states in our own times. If we do so, we shall find that they shared, first, a common weakness in regard to their military organizations, for the reasons fully discussed above. Then, it will be found that some of them incurred the hostility of the people or, if they had the people on their side, they did not know how to keep the allegiance of the nobles. If they are not undermined in one of these ways, states which are robust enough to keep an army in the field cannot be lost. Philip of Macedon (not the father of Alexander but the one who was conquered by Titus Quintius) ruled a minor dominion in comparison with the greatness of the Romans who attacked him with Greek auxiliaries. None the less, as he was a military man, who knew how to content the people and keep the allegiance of the nobles, he sustained the war against them for many years; and although at the end he lost control of some cities, he still kept his kingdom.

So these princes of ours, whose power had been established many years, may not blame fortune for their losses. Their own indolence was to blame, because, having never imagined when times were quiet that they could change (and this is a common failing of mankind, never to anticipate a storm when the sea is calm), when adversity came their first thoughts were of flight and not of resistance. They hoped that the people, revolted by the outrages of the conqueror, would recall them. Now this policy, when all else fails, is all to the good. But it is wrong to have neglected other precautions in that hope: we do not find men falling down just because they expect to find someone helping them up. It may not happen; and, if it does happen, it leaves you unsafe because your expedient was cowardly and not based on your own actions. The only sound, sure, and enduring methods of defence are those based on your own actions and prowess.

XXV

How far human affairs are governed by fortune, and how fortune can be opposed

I am not unaware that many have held and hold the opinion that events are controlled by fortune and by God in such a way that the prudence of men cannot modify them, indeed, that men have no influence whatsoever. Because of this, they would conclude that there is no point in sweating over things, but that one should submit to the rulings of chance. This opinion has been more widely held in our own times, because of the great changes and variations, beyond human imagining, which we have experienced and experience every day. Sometimes, when thinking of this, I have myself inclined to this same opinion. None the less, so as not to rule out our free will, I believe that it is probably true that fortune is the arbiter of half the things we do, leaving the other half or so to be controlled by ourselves. I compare fortune to one of those violent rivers which, when they are enraged, flood the plains, tear down trees and buildings, wash soil from one place to deposit it in another. Everyone flees before them, everybody yields to their impetus, there is no possibility of resistance. Yet although such is their nature, it does not follow that when they are flowing quietly one cannot take precautions, constructing dykes and embankments so that when the river is in flood they would keep to one channel or their impetus be less wild and dangerous. So it is with fortune. She shows her potency where there is no well-regulated power to resist her, and her impetus is felt where she knows there are no embankments and dykes built to restrain her. If you consider Italy, the theatre of those changes and variations I mentioned, which first appeared here, you will see that she is a country without embankments and without dykes: for if Italy had been adequately reinforced, like Germany, Spain, and France, either this flood would not have caused the great changes it has, or it would not have swept in at all.

I want what I have said to suffice, in general terms, on the question of how to oppose fortune. But, confining myself now to particular circumstances, I say that we see that some princes flourish one day and come to grief the next, without appearing to have changed in character or any other way. This I believe arises, first, for the reasons discussed at length earlier on, namely, that those princes who are utterly dependent on fortune come to grief when their fortune changes. I also believe that the one who adapts his policy to the times prospers, and likewise that the one whose policy clashes with the demands of the times does not. It can be observed that men use various methods in pursuing their own personal objectives, that is glory and riches. One man proceeds with circumspection, another impetuously; one uses violence, another stratagem; one man goes about things patiently, another does the opposite; and yet everyone, for all this diversity of method, can reach his objective. It can also be observed that with two circumspect men, one will achieve his end, the other not; and likewise two men succeed equally well with different methods, one of them being circumspect and the other impetuous.

This results from nothing else except the extent to which their methods are or are not suited to the nature of the times. Thus it happens that, as I have said, two men, working in different ways, can achieve the same end, and of two men working in the same way one gets what he wants and the other does not. This also explains why prosperity is ephemeral; because if a man behaves with patience and circumspection and the time and circumstances are such that this method is called for, he will prosper; but if time and circumstances change he will be ruined because he does not change his policy. Nor do we find any man shrewd enough to know how to adapt his policy in this way; either because he cannot do otherwise than what is in character or because, having always prospered by proceeding one way, he cannot persuade himself to change. Thus a man who is circumspect, when circumstances demand impetuous behaviour, is unequal to the task, and so he comes to grief. If he changed his character according to the time and circumstances, then his fortune would not change.

Pope Julius II was impetuous in everything; and he found the time and circumstances so favourable to his way of proceeding that he always met with success. Consider his first campaign, against Bologna, when messer Giovanni Bentivogli was still living. The Venetians mistrusted it: so did the king of Spain; and Julius was still arguing about the enterprise with France. None the less, with typical forcefulness and impetuosity, he launched the expedition in person. This move disconcerted and arrested Spain and the Venetians, the latter because they were afraid and the former because of the king's ambition to reconquer all the kingdom of Naples. On the other hand, he drew the king of France after him. This was because the king, seeing Julius go into action, and anxious for his support in subduing the Venetians, decided he could not refuse him troops without doing him a manifest disservice. With that impetuous move of his, therefore, Julius achieved what no other pontiff, with the utmost human prudence, would have achieved. Because had Julius delayed setting out from Rome until all his plans and negotiations were completed, as any other pontiff would have done, he would never have succeeded. The king of France would have found a hundred and one excuses, and the others would have inspired Julius with a hundred and one fears. I shall not discuss his other deeds, which were all like this and which all met with success. The brevity of his pontifical life did not let him experience the contrary. If there had come a time when it was necessary for him to act with circumspection he would have come to grief: he would never have acted other than in character.

I conclude, therefore, that as fortune is changeable whereas men are obstinate in their ways, men prosper so long as fortune and policy are in accord, and when there is a clash they fail. I hold strongly to this: that it is better to be impetuous than circumspect; because fortune is a woman and if she is to be submissive it is necessary to beat and coerce her. Experience shows that she is more often subdued by men who do this than by those who act coldly. Always, being a woman, she favours young men, because they are less circumspect and more ardent, and because they command her with greater audacity.

XXVI
Exhortation to liberate Italy from the barbarians

After deliberating on all the things discussed above, I asked myself whether in present-day Italy the times were propitious to honour a new prince, and whether the circumstances existed here which would make it possible for a prudent and capable man to introduce a new order, bringing honour to himself and prosperity to all the Italians. Well, I believe that so many things conspire to favour a new prince, that I cannot imagine there ever was a time more suitable than the present. And if, as I said, the Israelites had to be enslaved in Egypt for Moses to emerge as their forceful leader; if the Persians had to be oppressed by the Medes so that the greatness of Cyrus could be recognized; if the Athenians had to be scattered to demonstrate the excellence of Theseus: then, at the present time, in order to discover the worth of an Italian spirit, Italy had to be brought to her present extremity. She had to be more enslaved than the Hebrews, more oppressed than the Persians, more widely scattered than the Athenians; leaderless, lawless, crushed, despoiled, torn, overrun; she had to have endured every kind of desolation.

And although before now there was a man in whom some spark seemed to show that he was ordained by God to redeem the country, none the less it was seen how afterwards, at the very height of his career, he was rejected by fortune. So now, left lifeless, Italy is waiting to see who can be the one to heal her wounds, put an end to the sacking of Lombardy, to extortion in the Kingdom and in Tuscany, and cleanse those sores which have now been festering for so long. See how Italy beseeches God to send someone to save her from those barbarous cruelties and outrages; see how eager and willing the country is to follow a banner, if only someone will raise it. And at the present time it is impossible to see in what she can place more hope than in your illustrious House, which, with its fortune and prowess, favoured by God and by the Church, of which it is now the head, can lead Italy to her salvation. The task will not be very hard, if you will call to mind the actions and lives of the men I have mentioned. These men may be exceptional and remarkable; they were men none the less, and each of them had less opportunity than is offered now. Their enterprise was neither more just nor easier, and God was no more their friend than he is yours. There is great justice in our cause: '*iustum enim est bellum quibus necessarium, et pia arma ubi nulla nisi in armis spes est*'.* There is the greatest readiness, and where that is so there cannot be great difficulty, provided only your House will emulate the methods of those I have singled out for admiration. As well as this, unheard-of wonders are to be seen, performed by God: the sea is divided, a cloud has shown you the way, water has gushed from the rock, it has rained manna; all things have conspired to your greatness. The rest is up to you. God does not want to do everything Himself, and take away from us

---

* 'Because a necessary war is a just war and where there is hope only in arms, those arms are holy.'

our free will and our share of the glory which belongs to us.

It is not to be marvelled at that none of the Italians I have named has succeeded in doing what, it is hoped, your illustrious House will do, or that in so many revolutions in Italy and so many martial campaigns it has always seemed that our military prowess has been extinguished. This is because the old military systems were bad and there has been no one who knew how to establish a new one. And nothing brings a man greater honour than the new laws and new institutions he establishes. When these are soundly based and bear the mark of greatness, they make him revered and admired. Now, in Italy the opportunities are not wanting for thorough reorganization. Here we would find greater prowess among those who follow, were it not lacking among the leaders. Look at the duels and the combats between a few, how the Italians are superior in strength, in skill, in inventiveness; but when it is a matter of armies, they do not compare. All this is because of the weakness of the leaders. Those who are capable are not obeyed. Everyone imagines he is competent, and hitherto no one has had the competence to dominate the others by his prowess and good fortune. As a result of this, over so long a time, in so many wars during the past twenty years, when there has been an all-Italian army it has always given a bad account of itself, as witness the battles of Taro, then Alessandria, Capua, Genoa, Vailà, Bologna, and Mestre.

Therefore if your illustrious House wants to emulate those eminent men who saved their countries, before all else it is essential for it, as the right basis for every campaign, to raise a citizen army; for there can be no more loyal, more true, or better troops. Taken singly, these troops are good; acting as a united army, when they find themselves under the command of their own prince and honoured and maintained by him, they are still better. It is necessary, therefore, to raise such an army, in order to base our defence against the invaders on Italian strength. Although the Swiss and Spanish infantry may be considered formidable, none the less there are faults in both which would enable a third kind of army not only to hold them in battle but to be sure of conquering. The Spaniards cannot withstand cavalry, and the Swiss have cause to fear infantrymen who meet them in combat with a determination equal to their own. Thus it has been found, and experience will prove, that the Spaniards cannot withstand French cavalry and the Swiss succumb to Spanish infantry. There may have been no complete demonstration of this latter assertion, but there was some indication of its truth at the battle of Ravenna, where Spanish infantry troops clashed with the German battalions, which adopt the same line of battle as the Swiss. In the encounter, the Spaniards, making good use of their bucklers, with great agility thrust their way between and under the German pikes, and attacked with impunity while the Germans were defenceless. If it had not been for the cavalry which charged them, the Spaniards would have annihilated the Germans. So, having grasped the defects of these Swiss and Spanish infantry, you can develop a new type, capable of withstanding cavalry and undaunted by other infantry. This will be ensured by raising new armies and employing new formations. It is things of this kind which, when newly introduced, bring a new prince greatness and prestige.

In order therefore that Italy, after so long a time, may behold its saviour, this opportunity must not be let slip. And I cannot express with what love he would be welcomed in all those provinces which have suffered from these foreign inundations, with what thirst for vengeance, with what resolute loyalty, with what devotion and tears. What doors would be closed to him? What people would deny him their obedience? What envy should stand in his way? What Italian would refuse him allegiance? This barbarous tyranny stinks in everyone's nostrils. Let your illustrious House undertake this task, therefore, with the courage and hope which belong to just enterprises, so that, under your standard, our country may be ennobled, and under your auspices what Petrarch said may come to pass:

> Vertue 'gainst fury shall advance the fight,
> And it i' th' combate soone shall put to flight:
> For th' old Romane valour is not dead,
> Nor in th' Italians brests extinguished.